THE ATLANTIC CRITICAL STUDIES

John Webster's

The Duchess of Malfi

RATRI RAY

ATLANTIC

PUBLISHERS & DISTRIBUTORS (P) LTD

Published by

ATLANTIC

PUBLISHERS & DISTRIBUTORS (P) LTD

7/22, Ansari Road, Darya Ganj, New Delhi-110002
Phones : +91-11-40775252, 40775214, 23273880, 23275880
Fax : +91-11-23285873
Web : www.atlanticbooks.com
E-mail : orders@atlanticbooks.com

Branch Office: Chennai
Phones : +91-44-48531784, 28291383
E-mail : chennai@atlanticbooks.com

Printed & bound in India by Atlantic Print Services

General Preface

The study-aids available in England and America, among other places, form the basis of *The Atlantic Critical Studies* which is primarily meant to cater to the needs of the students of English Literature in Indian universities.

The students in India pursuing English Honours and Post-graduation in English have to study under various constraints like non-availability of relevant critical books, dearth of foreign and Indian journals, inaccessibility to good and well-equipped libraries, among others. Although internet is of great help to the students these days, yet the plethora of information it brings before them often confuses them and they end up choosing a lot of irrelevant material which shifts the focus away from the topic or theme under discussion.

The books under *The Atlantic Critical Studies* fill the gap between the requirements and availability, and help the students by providing them quality material pertinent to their academic pursuits.

The series covers authors and works that are widely prescribed in Indian universities. This was necessary considering a regular demand for books that critically examine these authors and their works. The books in this series discuss all the major aspects of the works, besides providing sufficient information on the authors and the period in which they wrote. This makes each book in the series self-sufficient and of great benefit to the students. The scholarly authors who have prepared the books in the series have used authentic sources and taken special care to combine lucidity and profundity in their treatment of the texts.

The References in each chapter and the Select Bibliography at the end of the book are meant to help the students in making further study in specific areas if they want to.

The books under *The Atlantic Critical Studies* will also help researchers besides students and teachers of English Literature.

Ratri Ray

Introduction

John Webster is one of the youngest contemporaries of Shakespeare, so he is regarded as being more of a Jacobean than an Elizabethan. He was born only six years after Shakespeare and died about eighteen years after him, so this view is justified. Dramatists such as Shakespeare, Ben Jonson, Webster, Tourneur, Beaumont, and Fletcher belonged, with a few years' difference, to the same period, the Golden Age of English Literature, i.e., the Elizabethan-Jacobean Age which was very rich in every way as will be seen in the chapters that follow—in geographical expansion, economic growth, industrial growth, political stability, etc. But, for the student of literature, it is specially known as the Golden Age of English Literature. Every aspect of English Literature underwent a growth and development unprecedented before and unequalled afterwards in—drama, narrative poetry, lyrics, discursive prose, fiction—every field. There were subtle differences between the mental attitudes of the two ages—the former was enthusiastic, ebullient, expansive, and the latter was more pessimistic and contemplative. This is reflected in the literature of the two periods also. For example, all of Shakespeare's plays up to the Golden Comedies (*The Merchant of Venice, As You Like It,* and *Twelfth Night*) are products of Elizabethan Age and the tragedies and the later plays were written in the Jacobean Age. There are many more such examples. Sir John Davies's philosophical poem *Nosce Teipsum* gives the prevailing mood:

> And to conclude, I know myself a MAN
> which is a proud and yet a wretched being.[1]

The very thought of man and the world and their relationship, in other words, was based on doubt and pessimism; and Webster's plays, specially *The Duchess of Malfi,* reflect this mentality.

This is not to say that cheerful literature was not produced during the time at all. To take Webster only, he collaborated with Dekker on city comedies which were highly successful. Later in his life he also collaborated with Middleton, Rowley, and Heywood to produce city comedies. But it cannot be denied that the plays on which his reputation as a dramatist rests are his tragedies, brooding over evil in the nature of man and the universe. This aspect is highlighted the most by modern critics. W.A. Edwards wrote of Webster in 1933:

> Events are not within control, nor are our human desires; let's snatch what comes and clutch it, fight our way out of tight corners, and meet the end without squealing.[2]

References

1. Quoted in Spencer, T. *Shakespeare and the Nature of Man*, Cambridge Univ. Press, 1945, p. 28.
2. *Scrutiny* '33-'34. Quoted in Internet material on Webster, p. 2.

Contents

The Atlantic Critical Studies

D.H. Lawrence's *Sons and Lovers* by *Atlantic Research Division*, pp. 168, ₹ 495.00

E.M. Forster's *A Passage to India* by *Rama Kundu*, pp. 296, 2007, ₹ 550.00

Emily Brontë's *Wuthering Heights* by *Jibesh Bhattacharyya*, pp. 192, ₹ 350.00

Ernest Hemingway's *A Farewell to Arms* by *P.G. Rama Rao*, pp. 168, ₹ 350.00

Ernest Hemingway's *The Old Man and the Sea* by *P.G. Rama Rao*, pp. 160, ₹ 395.00

Jane Austen's *Pride and Prejudice* by *Jibesh Bhattacharyya*, pp. 192, ₹ 350.00

Joseph Conrad's *Heart of Darkness* by *Mohit Kumar Ray*, pp. 208, ₹ 495.00

Ruth Prawer Jhabvala's *Heat and Dust* by *I.H. Shihan*, pp. 160, ₹ 350.00

Salman Rushdie's *Midnight's Children* by *Pradip Kumar Dey*, pp. 168, ₹ 395.00

William Golding's *Lord of the Flies* by *Santwana Haldar*, pp. 184, ₹ 495.00

William Shakespeare's *Antony and Cleopatra* by *Ratri Ray*, pp. 208, ₹ 495.00

William Shakespeare's *Othello* by *Jibesh Bhattacharyya*, pp. 232, ₹ 450.00

William Shakespeare's *The Merchant of Venice* by *Ratri Ray*, pp. 184, ₹ 375.00

William Shakespeare's *A Midsummer Night's Dream* by *Ratri Ray*, pp. 192, ₹ 395.00

William Shakespeare's *As You Like It* *by Ratri Ray*, pp. 200, ₹ 450.00

William Shakespeare's *Hamlet* by *Ratri Ray*, pp. 216, ₹ 495.00

William Shakespeare's *Julius Caesar* by *Ratri Ray*, pp. 200, ₹ 495.00

William Shakespeare's *King Lear* by *Ratri Ray*, pp. 184, ₹ 395.00

William Shakespeare's *Othello* by *Ratri Ray*, pp. 208, ₹ 395.00

William Shakespeare's *The Tempest* by *Ratri Ray*, pp. 192, ₹ 395.00

William Shakespeare's *Twelfth Night* by *Ratri Ray*, pp. 224, ₹ 395.00

William Shakespeare's *Macbeth* by *Ratri Ray*, pp. 162, ₹ 495.00

Christopher Marlowe's *Dr. Faustus* by *Ratri Ray*, pp. 134, ₹ 495.00

1
The Background

(A) THE SOCIO-POLITICAL BACKGROUND

It is true that Webster did not see much of the Elizabethan Age. Yet it is advisable to begin our sketch of the socio-political background with the accession of Queen Elizabeth since it gives us a complete picture of the Elizabethan Age and continue till the death of Webster.

A literary artist cannot be isolated from his background and Webster was as integrally connected with his background as anyone else. G.M. Trevelyan says with authority about Shakespeare what can be said about Webster also:

> His works could never have been produced in any other period than those late Elizabethan and early Jacobean times in which it was his luck to live. He could not have written as he did if the men and women among whom his days were passed had been other than they were.[1]

Before starting to study any writer, it is necessary, thus, to know the socio-political background of his time. Webster's lifespans a most eventful time in the history of England—the end of the sixteenth and the first quarter of the seventeenth centuries. A brief chronological table of the relevant years is given here. It contains the main political, social and religious events up till Webster's death.

A Chronological Table 1574–1634

1574 – Burbage gets licence for the first theatre in London.

'76 – Tycho Brahe begins his astronomical studies.

– Burbage opens the first theatre.

'77 – Treaty with the Dutch signed. Sir Francis Drake begins his circumnavigation of the world.

'80 – Webster born.

– Sir Francis Drake completes circumnavigation.

'81 – Conversion to Roman Catholicism declared to be a treasonable act.

– Galileo discovers the Law of the Pendulum.

'83 – Plot against the Queen.

– Humphrey Gilbert takes possession of Newfoundland for England.

'84 – Sir Walter Raleigh discovers Virginia, names and colonizes it.

'86 – England wins the battle of Zutphen in which Sir Philip Sidney dies.

– Plot against the Queen. Mary Queen of the Scots convicted of treason.

'87 – Rose Theatre built by Henslowe.

'88 – Defeat of the Spanish Armada by Drake.

'89 – Galileo publishes the results of his experiment with falling bodies.

'92 – John Davis discovers the Falkland Islands.

'93 – Absence from the Church on Sundays made punishable by law.

'95 – Southwell the poet executed for celebrating Mass.

'96 – England, France and Netherlands form an alliance against Spain.

'97 – Statutory provision made for Poor Relief and beggary made illegal.

'98 – The Bodleian Library begun. Globe Theatre opened.

1603 – Queen Elizabeth dies. King James-I succeeds.

'04 – Peace with Spain achieved by the King.

– Acts against priests and recusants. Anglican canons made and enforced.

’05 – Repression of Puritans and Catholics. Gunpowder plot by Guy Fawkes.

’08 – Failure of plan for union with Scotland.

’10 – Judicial decision against royal proclamations.

’11 – Parliament dissolved by the King.

’12 – Alliance with German Protestant princes.

– Witches hanged at Lancaster.

’13 – Elizabeth daughter of King James marries Elector Frederick V of Germany.

’14 – King James summons “Addled Parliament”, the members quarrel with him.

’16 – England returns to Netherlands the towns of Flushing and Brill.

– The King dismisses the Chief Justice for repeated failure to give judgement in his favour.

’17 – The King meets Scots Parliament.

– Ben Jonson granted royal pension.

– Sir Walter Raleigh fails to find El Dorado.

’19 – Elector Frederick, the King’s son-in-law, becomes the King. James I refuses to help him.

’21 – King James rebukes Parliament for daring to criticise his plan to marry his heir Prince Charles to a Spanish Princess. Parliament replies with the “Great Protestation”, setting out its rights.

’22 – King James dismisses Parliament and imprisons three members. Negotiations of Anglo-Spanish royal marriage resumed.

’24 – France and England sign treaty for the marriage of Prince Charles to Henrietta Maria, sister of Louis XIII.

’25 – King James dies. Succeeded by Charles I.

’34 – Webster dies.

This table presents a fairly clear picture of the contemporary socio-political situation. The Queen was a tolerant ruler as far as religion was concerned and slowly but steadily, she brought peace and prosperity to the country. She was:

> to her subjects the symbol of their
> unity, prosperity and freedom.[2]

Trevelyan has declared that the establishing of a definite religion in England was one of her greatest achievements. Her religious policy came to prosper for it reached the heart of the England attitude:

> an attitude to religion that is not primarily Catholic or Protestant, Puritan or Anglican, but which evades dogma and lives broadly in the spirit.[3]

So far as the social hierarchy was concerned, class barriers existed but did not give rise to resentment anywhere. The feudal lords were usually conscientious and did not suppress the lower classes. Constant changes existed in the classes as G.M. Trevelyan perceives:

> Class division, recognised without fuss on either side, were no rigid and were not strictly hereditary. Individuals and families moved out of one class into another by acquisition or loss of property, or by simple change of occupation.[4]

Each individual was entitled to a fair wage by honest labour. This led to self-respect and self-reliance. There were no bondmen or slaves. Hard work was done, but it was paid for. "Honest labour bears a lovely face."

Innovation in the industrial field was a feature of the times. The factory system gave a new measure of efficiency and the capitalist owner was proud of his productivity. Mining had extended to lead, copper, tin and iron which had not been available so easily earlier. Now they were, to everyone.

Sir Francis Drake gave a boost to national pride by succeeding in two famous deeds—the defeat of the Spanish Armada and the circumnavigation of the globe. This sense of joy, security and pride can be seen in literature too.

The colonising of foreign places was another feature of the time. King James made peace with Spain in the first year of his reign which made the seas safe and settlers started to colonise the new foreign lands like Virginia, etc. Hakluyt's book was of great importance in this context:

> Hakluyt, in narrating the deeds of our explorers and seamen, directed across the ocean the thoughts of adventurous youths, of scholars, statesmen and merchants, and of all who had money to invest.[5]

But Webster lived till the end of King James's reign and a few years into the Caroline Age. As can be seen in the table given above these years of King James's reign are not very peaceful ones and justifies the pessimistic spirit of the age. The King tried again and again to bring about the union of Scotland and England and failed every time. In the end he got angry with the Parliament, dissolving it again and again and started behaving like a dictator. All this was reflected in the literature of the period and in Webster because the best plays of Webster were written during this time. The spirit was caught by his readers of modern times as is reflected in the quotation given earlier (*vide* Introduction, quotation by W.A. Edwards). The furious causes and grand illusions of those days are like the ghosts of worn, vanquished mountain ranges, now sunk beneath the seas of history.

(B) The Literary Background

The Elizabethan Age is known as the Golden Age—and not for nothing. It was a prosperous one from all points of view, social, political or literary. A chronological table is given below. It begins with the publication of *Shepheardes Calendar* and ends with Webster's death.

A Chronological Table 1579–1634

1579 – *Shepheardes Calender* by Spenser.

'85 – Kyd's *The Spanish Tragedy*.

'86 – Sir Philip Sidney dies. Lyly's *Endymion*.

'87 – Marlowe's *Tamburlaine*, Lyly's *Gallathea*.

'89 – Marlowe's *Jew of Malta*.

'90 – *The Faerie Queene Bks* I-III (pub.).

'91 – Sidney's *Astrophel and Stella*, Daniel's *To Delia*, Shakespeare's *Comedy of Errors*.

'92 – Revised *Arcadia, Arden of Faversham.*

'93 – Shakespeare's *Richard III, Romeo and Juliet, Venus and Adonis.*

'94 – Shakespeare's *Rape of Lucrece*, the sonnets, *Timon of Athens.*

'95 – *Amoretti, Epithalamion, Apologie for Poetry, Richard II, A Midsummer Night's Dream, Love's Labour's Lost, King John, Taming of the Shrew.*

'98 – Marlowe's *Hero and Leander*, Shakespeare's *Henry IV Pt II, Merry Wives of Windsor.*

'99 – Spenser dies. *Henry V, Much Ado About Nothing, Julius Caesar.*

1600 – *England's Helicon*, Ben Jonson's Cynthia's Revels, Shakespeare's *As You Like It, Twelfth Night.*

'01 – Dekker and Marston's *Satiromastix*, Jonson *Poetaster.*

'02 – *Hamlet, Troilus and Cressida, All's Well That Ends Well* (all by Shakespeare).

'03 – *Sejanus, A Woman Killed with Kindness.*

'04 – Chapman's *Bussy D'Ambois*, Marston's *The Malcontent, Measure for Measure, Othello.*

'05 – Middleton's *A Trick to Catch the Old One, King Lear.*

'06 – Lyly dies, *Yorkshire Tragedy*, Jonson's *Volpone*, Tourneur's *The Revenger's Tragedy, Macbeth.*

'07 – Beaumont and Fletcher's *Knight of the Burning Pestle, Antony and Cleopatra.*

'08 – Fuller and Milton born. *Coriolanus, Timon of Athens, Pericles, the Prince of Tyre* (all by Shakespeare).

'09 – *Philaster*, Fulke Greville's *Mustapha.*

'10 – Jonson's *The Alchemist, Cymbeline, The Winter's Tale, The Tempest* (all three by Shakespeare).

'11 – *The Authorised Version of the Bible. Henry VIII.*

’12 – Crashaw born, Chapman’s *Iliad I-XXIV*, Donne’s *The Second Anniversarie*, Webster *The White Devil.*

’13 – Constable and Overbury die. Purchas’s *Pilgrimage.*

’14 – Overbury’s *Characters*, Lodge’s *Works of Seneca*, Jonson’s *Bartholomew Fair*, Webster’s *The Duchess of Malfi.*

’16 – Shakespeare dies, Jonson’s *Epicene.*

’17 – Jonson granted royal pension.

’19 – Beaumont and Fletcher’s *The Maid’s Tragedy*, *A King and no King.*

’21 – Burton’s *Anatomy of Melancholy.*

’24 – Middleton’s *A Game of Chess.*

’25 – Jonson’s *The Staple of News*, Bacon’s *Essays.*

’26 – Bacon *New Atlantis*, Sandys’s translation of Ovid’s *Metamorphoses.*

’29 – Milton’s *Nativity* ode.

’30 – Dekker’s *The Honest Whore* Pt. 2, Galilei’s *Dialogue* on Ptolemaic and Copernican System.

’33 – Milton’s *L’Allegro* and *II Penseroso.*

’34 – Webster dies.

It is perfectly true that the years given here are the best years of this Elizabethan-cum-Jacobean age. Only a few of the works written during this time have been mentioned above, the stress falling on drama. Many prose works had also been published, as well as lyrics and sonnets. Many of them have not been mentioned for it is not possible to give all of them, nor have the authors been always named.

It has been said by Hardin Craig, a noted authority on the period:

> The characteristic and most distinguished form that literature assumed in renaissance England was drama.[6]

In the field of sonnets, songs and narrative poems the situation is a bit better. Spenser’s *Shepheardes Calender* and the first few books of *The Faerie Queene* the sonnets of the Earls of Wyatt and of Surrey had been published by Tottel in his famous *Miscellany* but we are not much interested in them, or in the sonnet-sequences, as Webster was not interested. The main theme of the songs, as of the sonnet-sequences, is light-hearted love:

> The song-lyric, as developed in accord with the musical art of the time, is too light an instrument to utter the deeper notes of passion, and its theme is fanciful love, love that laughs and entreats.[7]

One of the most famous songs of the time, Webster's "Call for the robin red-breast" however, has nothing to do with love of any kind.

Our immediate concern is drama. Kyd's famous play *The Spanish Tragedy* was a revenge tragedy in the Senecan mode. This famous play was taken as a model for later revenge tragedies. *Tamburlaine*, a conqueror tragedy was so popular that Marlowe had to write a sequel to it. Burbage and Henslowe founded theatre halls and the dramatists experimented with different kinds of drama. In their hands the five-act drama branched out into many directions. There were four kinds of tragedies and comedies too were of many different kinds. In addition, there were the chronicles and light works like farces and masques. Shakespeare, Ben Jonson, Marlowe, Kyd, Webster, Tourneur, Chapman, Beaumont and Fletcher, Middleton, Marston—these are some of the prominent names.

Seneca was the model for tragedies and they came to be known as the "blood-and-thunder" tragedies. These have been classified into four kinds: Conqueror tragedy, like Marlowe's *Tamburlaine*, the Revenge tragedy, like Kyd's *The Spanish Tragedy*, Villain tragedy like *The Changeling* by Middleton and Rowley, and the Domestic tragedy like the anonymous *Arden of Faversham*. The categories are not mutually exclusive and one play can have the features of other kinds also. Our poet's *Duchess of Malfi* for example, can be labelled as a domestic tragedy and a revenge one.

Comedy, of many different kinds, flourished in the hands of the many playwrights, Shakespeare himself wrote comedies of different types. Jonson wrote humour comedies, Webster wrote comedies in collaboration with others. They were satirical city comedies. Beaumont and Fletcher wrote tragicomedies.

There were numerous farces, providing boisterous, healthy entertainment. These, like the satirical comedies, dealt with non-aristocratic characters. Shakespeare's *The Merry Wives of Windsor* has become famous as it was specially commissioned by the Queen, who wanted to see "the fat knight in love".

Masques were a different kind of entertainment. They were very popular, used for celebrating happy occasions like betrothals, weddings, etc. They used mythical and supernatural characters like nymphs, satyrs, gods, etc. They were expensive productions using gorgeous costumes, etc. So, they were used at Court and in aristocratic houses. Jonson wrote many masques.

This brief account will scarcely serve to bring home to the reader the rich wealth of Elizabethan-Jacobean drama. These plays were all extremely stage-worthy and everybody involved made their livings out of them. M.C. Bradbrook, in a pithy sentence, says:

> Security, stability and easiness had been achieved, and the particular linguistic problems which vexed the previous generation could never re-occur. The English tongue was now capable of eloquence, and their language was to the generation that followed "our nation's best glory".[8]

But this glory of the English language that M.C. Bradbrook mentions here (without giving any examples) cannot be understood by the student unless and until some examples are given. In every field of literature, there was copious and rich variety. Each genre had its own rich products. We are specially interested only in one aspect of it, tragic drama, but though this itself is rich enough it does not give any idea of the variety and excellence of the literary background as a whole. Shakespeare, by himself, provides examples of tragedy, comedy, and history in drama. His narrative poems give examples of that genre, his sonnets provide examples from sonnets and his numerous songs give examples of lyric poetry. All this—from the work of just one author, and what of the whole galaxy of writers among whom, admittedly, Shakespeare was the brightest star. A few examples are given below of the literary work of the period in different genres, as far as possible, from the words of poets other than Shakespeare, though a few examples will be taken from him too. This is being done in order to give the student an idea of the general excellence of the work of the period. The work of just one author is not enough for this purpose.

Thus, to start with, let us take drama. In tragedy, as explained above, we have Kyd, Marlowe, Webster himself, Tourneur and others. Here are two examples from Marlowe (who is the epitome for Conqueror tragedy) to illustrate two kinds of poetry. First, we have the Marlovian grand manner:

> And ride in triumph through Persepolis!
> Is it not brave to be a king, Techelles,
> Usumcasane and Theridamas?
> Is it not passing brave to be a king,
> And ride in triumph through Persepolis?
> .... To be a king is half to be a god
> .... A god is not so glorious as a king.[9]

This is in the well-known Marlovian grand manner, but he can be tender and musical when, and if, he wants:

> Zenocrate, the loveliest maid alive;
> Fairer than rocks of pearl and precious stone,
> The only paragon of Tamburlaine;
> Whose eyes are brighter than the lamps of heaven
> And speech more pleasant than sweet harmony.[10]

But far more important, really, than all these are those passages in which he approaches conversational rhythm in blank verse, which is an extremely difficult thing to do:

> Mountains and hills, come, come, and fall on me,
> And hide me from the heavy wrath of God.
> No, no!
> Then will I head long run into the earth
> Earth, gape. O no, it will not harbour me.[11]

In narrative poetry there is, of course, *Venus and Adonis* by Shakespeare the sensuality of which is celebrated. Marlowe too wrote one narrative poem and he left that unfinished. But for sheer fancifulness and musical beauty here is a passage that describes a part of Hero's skirt, of the dress she wore formally as a priestess:

> And branch'd with blushing coral to the knee,
> where sparrows perch'd, of hollow pearl and gold
> such as the world would wonder to behold.
> Those with sweet water oft her handmaid fills,
> which as she went would chirrup through the bills.[12]

We can take up the song-lyrics next. There is profusion of, and great variety in, the song-lyrics of the age, as has been noted by many different scholars. Carpenter's comment, a very pertinent one, has already been quoted. There is serious poetry to be seen in Sir Thomas Wyatt's famous poem:

> Forget not yet the tried intent
> Of such a truth as I have meant;
> My great travail so gladly spent,
> Forget not yet![13]

But this does not mean that all lyrics were as serious as this. In fact, most of them were quite light-hearted. One such is to be found in Udall's *Ralph Roister Doister*, one of the first light comedies:

> Pipe, merry Annot,
> Trilla, Trilla, Trillary.
> Work, Tibet; work, Annot; work, Margery
> Sew, Tibet; knit, Annot; spin, Margery
> Let us see who will win the victory.[14]

It is difficult to exclude any of the lyrics, as they serve to illustrate some quality or other. Let us have a few from Shakespeare to illustrate certain important features. Shakespeare, like the sun itself, shines on everyone and everything. So he writes about humble creatures in *A Midsummer Night's Dream*:

> You spotted snakes with double tongue,
> Thorny hedgehogs, be not seen;
> Newts and blind-worms, do no wrong
> Come not near our fairy queen.[15]

Neglecting the scores of other poets, let us look at those extremely significant lines from *The Tempest*:

> Full fathom five thy father lies
> ....
> Nothing of him that doth fade
> But doth suffer a sea-change
> Into something rich and strange.[16]

After these superb lines, there is little more to be said about the lyrics.

When we come to the sonnets, Shakespeare, of course, reigns supreme. But before we turn to him, it will be a crime not to mention Sir Philip Sidney and some others. There is an extremely serious, almost religious, sonnet by Sidney:

> Leave me, O Love, who reachest but to dust;
> And thou, my heart, aspire to higher things.
> Then, farewell, world; thy uttermost I see:
> Eternal Love, maintain thy life in me.[17]

Now let us turn to Shakespeare, who is a class by himself. He wrote a sequence of 154 sonnets, some addressed to his patron and some to the unknown Dark Lady, all revealing the inmost feeling of his heart. It is not possible to illustrate the many different qualities revealed by the sonnets—they have been studied intensively and extensively by Shakespearean scholars. Here only a few examples will be given. Here is one illustrating the permanence of poetry and of love:

> So long as men can breathe, or eyes can see
> So long lives this, and this gives life to thee.[18]

A.O. Lovejoy remarks about these lines that there is a "wonderful burst of splendour" in the tautology of these lines; that is, in the repetition of "so long." Now only one more example from the Dark Lady sonnets about the bitterness that is inherent in sensual love:

> Th' expense of spirit in a waste of shame
> Is lust in action....
> All this the world well knows, yet none knows well
> To shun the heaven that leads men to this hell.[19]

Now we have had examples from tragedy, narrative poetry, song lyrics and sonnets, but comedy is still left. Here also there is richness, complexity and variety. Ben Jonson alone, by himself, can provide us with many different examples of style, from grand to slang, and of different techniques also. Volpone's opening speech in the play named after him is a magnificent example, not of just grand style, but of an *aubade*, the opposite of a serenade. A few lines will be enough:

> Hail the world's soul and mine! More glad than is
> The teeming earth to see the longed-for sun
> Peep through the horns of the celestial Ram,
> Am I, to view thy splendour, darkening his;[20]

For grand style we cannot do better than turn to Sir Epicure Mammon in *The Alchemist*:

> I will have all my beds blown up, not stuffed:
> Down is too hard; and then, mine oval room
> Filled with such pictures as Tiberius took
> From Elephantis, and dull Aretine
> But coldly imitated.[21]

But it is not in these obviously poetic passages that we see the actual glory of the style of the comedies of the Elizabethan-Jacobean Age. Paradoxically, it is in the conversational, even slangy, style that we see the comic style in its full glory and nobody has done better than Ben Jonson in this field. This is how Subtle and Face are quarrelling in *The Alchemist*:

> Thou vermin, have I ta'en thee out of dung,
> So poor, so wretched, when no living thing
> Would keep thee company, but a spider or worse?[22]

This is the best of "low" style, racy and slangy.

As far as technique is concerned, it is in this play that we can see an extreme example of stichomythia. This occurs when a line of blank verse (five iambic pentameter feet) is split up into several parts, between two or more persons. The example occurs in the play already quoted from, when Jonson splits up one blank verse line between just three persons, but it is split up six times:

Face: Bawd!
Subtle: Cowherd!
Face: Conjurer!
S. : Cut-purse!
F.: Witch!
Dol Common: O me![23]

This is a technique adopted in blank verse to give it the flexibility of conversation and Ben Jonson's example is an extreme one. It serves an added purpose: that of inducing laughter which is necessary in comedies.

Apart from poetry and drama there is prose and Elizabethan-Jacobean prose is not any less rich than its poetry. Webster himself used prose in his plays, as indeed, nearly all the dramatists did. This will be explained and analysed in the proper place. But Webster was not a prose artist and there were many serious prose artists in that age, giving examples of many different kinds of prose. This, indeed, it certainly is, part of its glory as M.C. Bradbrook had said. In this place examples would be given from only two such writers, of the classic "Attic" prose and of complex but poetic prose. The best example of the first kind is Bacon, from whose essay an example is being given now:

> Certainly there be that delight in giddiness, | and count it a bondage to fix a belief; || affecting free-will in thinking, | as well as in acting. ||[24]

This sentence can be divided into several parts, and those divisions can be further subdivided. This is a special technique of such style, balancing of parts of a sentence. In the sentence that has been quoted above there are two major parts only, which have been marked with double vertical lines and those parts are sub-divided into two more parts which have been marked with single vertical lines. Such divisions can be multiplied the sentence happens to be longer.

Sir Thomas Browne's prose is of a complex, different type. It is complicated, rhythmical, and poetical prose. An example is being given here from his "Religio Medici," which is known as his "spiritual autobiography."

> For my Religion, though there be several Circumstances that might persuade the Light-hearted I have none at all, (as the general scandal of my Profession, the natural course of my Studies, the indifferency of my Behavior and Discourse in matters of Religion, neither violently Defending one, nor with that common oddour and contention Opposing another;) yet, in despight hereof, I dare without usurpation assume the honourable Stile of a Christian.[25]

This sentence, one and one only is too complex to be analysed here. He wrote more obviously poetic prose elsewhere. The passage beginning "What song the Sirens sang" is a typical example of his musically ornate prose.

Besides such well-known prose writers there is religious prose, as is to be found in Donne's "sermon". It is a very carefully constructed prose, following the principles given by classical writers of religious prose. His sermon on Death is a particularly well-known one.

Dramatic prose is an altogether different category. Here also, considerable variety is to be found, from rich poetic prose to the entirely conversational. Almost all the plays of the time were written in a mixture of prose and poetry. Webster's own dramatic prose, as has been said above will be explained and analysed in the proper place. There also, certain points about the use of prose in drama will be explained. In this place only a few examples will be given to illustrate the stability and glory, as M.C. Bradbrook had said, of Elizabethan Language. The example of pithy epigrammatic yet simple prose is given the best by Shakespeare in a famous sentence spoken by Malvolio in "Twelfth Night":

> Some are born great, some achieve greatness, and some have greatness thrust upon them.[26]

He provides many different varieties of dramatic prose from which no more examples are being given as the topic is but a minor one.

The above examples, it is hoped, have made it clear to the student what a rich literary background of prose, poetry and drama was there for Webster. He is firmly placed within this tradition for no writer can be separated from his tradition and he is definitely indebted to his own. Bradbrook's comment is fully to be credited, as the few examples given above have served to show.

References

1. Trevelyan, G.M., *Illustrated English Social History*, Vol. 2, Penguin Book Ltd., 1960, p. 125.
2. *Ibid.*, p. 15.
3. *Ibid.*, pp. 75-76.
4. *Ibid.*, p. 62.
5. *Ibid.*, p. 107.
6. Craig, Hardin, *The Literature of the English Renaissance: 1485-1660.* New York Collier Bks., 1950, p. 71.
7. Carpenter, F. Ives ed., *English Lyric Poetry: 1500-1700.* London, Blackie and Son Ltd., p. 47.
8. Bradbrook, M.C., *The Growth and Structure of Elizabethan Comedy*, London, Chatto and Windus, 1955, p. 41.
9. *Tamburlaine*, Pt I, Act II, sc v, ll. 50-57, from Pendry, E.D., ed. *Christopher Marlowe: Complete Plays and Poems*, Dent, London, 1976, p. 25.
10. *Tamburlaine* I, III: iii: 117-21, *ibid.*, p. 36.
11. *Dr. Faustus*, V: ii: 153-57, *ibid.*, p. 325.
12. *Hero and Leander*, ll. 32-37, *ibid.*, p. 401.
13. Carpenter, *op. cit.*, p. 5.
14. *Ibid.*, p. 12.
15. *Ibid.*, p. 81.
16. *Ibid.*, p. 87.
17. *Ibid.*, p. 48.
18. Booth, Stephen, ed., *Shakespeare's Sonnets*, New Haven and London, Yale Univ. Press, 1977, pp. 18-19.
19. *Ibid.*, pp. 110-11.
20. *Volpone*, Act I, sc. i, ll. 3-6 from Jamieson, M. ed., *Three Comedies: Ben Jonson*, Penguin, London, 1970 rpt., p. 51.
21. *The Alchemist*, II: ii: 41-45, *ibid.*, p. 219.
22. I : i : 65-67, *ibid.*, p. 195.
23. I : i : 107-12, *ibid.*, p. 197.

24. *Of Truth*, from Selby, F.G. ed., *Bacon's Essay*, Macmillan, 1971, London, p. 1.
25. *Sir Thomas Browne's Religio Medici*, Greenhill, W.A. ed., Macmillan & Co. Ltd., London, 1943, p. 7.
26. *Twelfth Night*, Act II, sc. v, ll. 160-61, Craig, W.J. ed., *The Complete Works of William Shakespeare*, London, Oxford Univ. Press, 1957 rpt., p. 309.

2
Life and Works

(A) WEBSTER'S LIFE (1580–1634)

The dates given above are doubtful. Not much is known about his life, either. In his own work *Monuments of Honour* he had added a preface in which he describes himself as "born free of the Merchant Taylors' Company". Scholars therefore think that he was the son of John Webster, a freeman of the guild of Merchant Taylors. He was probably what is known as the "cloth-worker" of the guild. Before this he was a carriage-maker and he was made free in 1571. Naturally, there is confusion in this, for some say that he was the son of a carriage-maker and some that he was a cloth-worker. Anyway, this means that he came of a prosperous and respectable middle-class level.

There is uncertainty about his school-life also. Possibly, he attended the Merchant Taylor's School and it is also possible that he might have been admitted at Middle Temple in 1598. He married Sara Peniall in 1605-06. Nothing of note is to be learnt about the next twenty years.

The first mention of his name in Henslowe's diary is in 1602 when, he along with Middleton, Drayton "and the rest" was paid for a lost play. All that is known about him after this is concerned with his work, little about his personal life. But this much is known: that a special licence had to be taken for his marriage with Sara for it was to take place during lent, and also because Sara was already seven months pregnant at the time. Their first child, a boy baby, was baptised at the parish of St. Dunstan-in-the-West. Other children were also born to him. A bequest by a neighbour who died in 1677 in his will signifies that certain other children were also there.

Webster went on writing till the mid-20s. Heywood in his *Hierarchy of the Blessed Angels* (1634) speaks of him in a way that indicates that by that time, 1634, he was dead. By such evidence as these a tentative biography has been arrived at by the scholars.

A Chronological Table of the Chief Events of his Life

1580 – ? Webster born

'86 – Possible date of admission into Merchant Taylor's School in Suffolk Lane, London.

'98 – "John Webster, lately of the New Inn" admitted to Middle Temple, one of the Inns of Court.

1602 – Started collaborating with other dramatists.

'04 – Worked with Dekker, Adapts Marston's *Malcontent.*

'05 – Worked with Dekker.

– First child John baptised at the parish of St. Dunstan in the West.

'06 – Married Sara Peniall.

'07 – Wrote *Sir Thomas Wyatt.*

'12 – *The White Devil* published and performed.

What is known of the rest of his life concerns his theatrical activities, i.e. the writing of and performance of his plays. These are given in the section on his works, so they are not repeated here.

(B) WEBSTER'S WORKS

Webster has written two of the best Jacobean tragedies, a tragicomedy, many city comedies in collaboration with other playwrights and sketches of characters. He also wrote a masque. Not much is known about most of the individual plays, many of them have been lost. A tentative chronological table is being given below:

A Chronological Table of his Works

1602 – *Caesar's Fall* (lost).

'04 – Induction to Marston's *The Malcontent.*

– Collaboration with Dekker in *Westward Ho*!

'05 – Collab with Dekker in *Northward Ho*!

'07 – *Sir Thomas Wyatt.*

'12 – *The White Devil.*

'14 – *The Duchess of Malfi.*

'15 – Contributed twenty-two character-sketches to Sir Thomas Overbury's *Characters.*

'21 – Collab. with Middleton in *Anything for a Quiet Life.*

'23 – *The Guise* (Lost). *The Devil's Law-Case.*

'24 – Collab. with Rowley in *A Cure for a Cuckold.*

– Mosque *Monument of Honour*, collab. with Ford, Rowley and Dekker in *Keep the Widow Waiting.*

Date uncertain—Collab. with Fletcher, Ford and Massinger in *Fair Maid of the Inn.*

Date uncertain—Collab. with Heywood *Appius and Virginia.*

Not much is known about many of the works of Webster except for the three major plays, *The White Devil, The Duchess of Malfi* and *The Devil's Law-Case.* Of them the first and the third will be commented upon here.

The White Devil

Emile Legouis relates this play to the series of studies of courtesans that had been written at that time, though this aspect has been neglected by modern critics. But, as Legouis pointed out, the play has got its roots implanted in the fertile soil of an entire series of such plays. All of them appeared one after another within a few years. The first of these was Marston's *The Dutch Courtezan.* Legouis includes Shakespeare's study of Cleopatra within the same tradition. Then there were Beaumont and Fletcher's *The Maid's Tragedy*, Middleton's *Women Beware Women* and Webster's *The White Devil.* All these plays were written in and around 1611.

Webster's play, thus, is not to be taken as an independent phenomenon. The play is remarkable for its portrayal of Vittoria who is a courtesan. She is taken from real life. Her licentious behaviour shocked even Rome at the end of the 16th century. She is the white devil of the title, beautiful, ambitious and very resourceful. She is the wife of a poor gentleman and is courted by Brachiano, the Duke of Padua. She convinces him that he must marry her but has to get rid of her husband and his wife first. Flamineo says about her:

> Excellent devil
> She hath taught him in a dream
> To make away his Duchess and her husband.[1]

Thus, a character in the play itself calls her a devil. The double murder is committed but those who profit by it are suspected. Vittoria is called before a court presided over by a Cardinal. Accusations and proofs are heaped upon her. She is so courageous and resourceful that she not only faces this imposing court but bravely manages to turn to nothing their accusations and proofs. The trial scene is truly an imposing one. Even then she is imprisoned and condemned to a confined life. But with the help of her lover she manages to escape. They are pursued and killed one after the other by the vengeful Duke of Florence. Vittoria manages to hold out by dint of her courage and cunning, but at last she is overcome. Even at the point of death she is haughty and brave. She is supported in all her misdeeds by her brother Flamineo, one of the most celebrated villains in Elizabethan literature.

This short summary is bad enough, but the details are worse and proof of Webster's morbid imagination. Brachiano's wife Isabella who is the very essence of purity, dies in a novel way: she is in the habit of kissing her husband's portrait every evening and this is poisoned. There is a scene in which a magician makes Brachiano see the double murder he has plotted. Brachiano's murder is done by pouring poison into a helmet which is then fixed to his head by an armourer. He dies in great pain while his enemies, disguised as holy friars reveal to him and tell him he is sure to be damned. It is difficult to say which scene is more sensational or melodramatic. Such incidents occur in almost every scene. It is, in addition, a play full of gorgeous spectacles. Legouis says:

> Never has there been a more perfect fusion of pure drama which is an effect of representing character and passion and melodrama, which is based on the horrors of physical impressions and on spectacular strangeness.[2]

The different aspects of the play have been judged from many different points of view. F.L. Lucas has observed that the Elizabethan dramatists were not concerned so much with plot as with scenes that were "a succession of great moments" and of "great situations ablaze with passion and poetry". But Ornstein observes that:

> All things considered, the plot of *The White Devil* is not more episodic than that of *King Lear*; it seems more episodic because *The White Devil* lacks the moral emphasis and focus which unifies the sprawling structure of Shakespeare's play.[3]

One thing is certain: this play contains much of Webster's best poetry as far as imagery and rhetoric and sheer poetic beauty is concerned. There are the celebrated lines that Isabella speaks to Brachiano:

> You have oft for these lips
> Neglected cassia and the natural sweets
> Of the spring violet. They are not yet much withered.[4]

Then again, when Brachiano blames Vittoria for his own downfall he says to her:

> Your beauty! O, then thousand curses on't.
> How long have I beheld the devil in crystal.
> Thou hast led me, like a heathen sacrifice
> With music and with fatal yokes of flower
> To my eternal ruin.[5]

Finally, there is the view that the art of the Elizabethans, according to Eliot, is an impure art:

> The art of the Elizabethans is an impure art.... The aim of the Elizabethans was to attain complete realism without

> surrendering any of the advantages which as artists they obeyed in unrealistic conventions.[6]

This is perfectly true of this play as is apparent from the instances of horror piled upon horror as given above, that followed the conventions of contemporary plays.

There is no doubt about the morality of the play. It is perfectly clear what the writer's moral attitude is. The idea portrayed here is one of evil that is all-pervasive. It is mostly in the character of Vittoria that this evil resides. As A. Nicoll has remarked:

> ...a woman Vittoria Corombona who might be accepted almost as a feminine counterpart of the Marlovian hero—prepared to indulge in every crime in order to achieve her ambitious ends.[7]

This remark succinctly sums up the morality of the play as well as its characters.

The Devil's Law-Case

This play (?1617-19) is the third play which is Webster's own work, i.e. written without collaboration. It is a tragicomedy and many critics think that he was influenced by Ben Jonson in it. There are certain scenes in it, specially the trial scene at the end in which Ornstein suggests that Webster had gone back to Marlowe's *The Jew of Malta* via the trial scene of Ben Jonson's *Volpone*. But in many ways it cannot be compared with *The White Devil* or *The Duchess of Malfi*, specially in its portrayal of characters. Its Machiavellian hero Romelio is always plotting and planning but cannot stand beside Flamineo and Bosola in depth. This is the opinion of Ornstein:

> ...its Machiavellian hero, Romelio, is too bourgeois to stand beside Flamineo or Bosola, and his engaging cynical candour is almost always completely submerged in the cross-currents of a swirling plot.[8]

This might easily be the result of Webster's attitude to the world he portrays in the play: it is one of derision to this infinitely venal world. He is impatient with the petty imbroglios the individual characters indulge in. Leonora for example awakens from her own illusions about her past. In a moment of excruciating vision, she remarks to her maid in what is one of the greatest passages not only in Webster but in entire Jacobean dramatic poetry including Shakespeare:

> Thou hast lived with me
> These forty years, we have grown old together,
> As many ladies with their women do
> With talking nothing and with doing less:
> We have spent our life in that which least concerns life
> Only in putting on our clothes.[9]

This is one of the most impressive passages in the dramatic poetry of the age. Yet, as Ornstein observes, Webster does not have the tolerance with which Shakespeare appreciates the bitter-sweet quality of human nature. Ornstein remarks:

> He lived in such imaginative communion with death that perhaps he could not respond to the beauty of spring without remembering the mockery and the beauty of a decked hearse.[10]

Una Ellis-Fermor, in her highly illuminating study of Webster, has many valuable observations to make which will be dealt with in the following chapters. Here only her observation on Webster's characters will be touched upon, as Ornstein does not have a very high opinion of Romelio's character as has been already referred to above. According to Ellis-Fermor Webster's characters, each of them, can be treated as belonging to a series. He has studied the same character differently in the three plays, *The White Devil, The Duchess of Malfi*, and *The Devil's Law-Case*. He has studied the character of villains in the same manner. Instead of calling such characters "villains" she call them "politicians." Flamineo in *The White Devil* is the first, then in *The Duchess of Malfi* there are two such characters, the Cardinal, and Bosola. About Romelio in this play she observes that in him Machiavellianism in not the result of planning, everything is just natural in him, even evil itself:

> Romelio in *The Devil's Law-Case*, the spontaneous, unanalytical but practical Machiavellianism...to offer at least one consistent and coherent explanation of man's

experience and destiny, he examines minutely a related series of figures that represent it.[11]

References

1. Quoted by H.T. Price in *Elizabethan Drama*, Kaufmann R.J. ed., p. 230.
2. Legouis, E. and Cazamian, L., *A History of English Literature*, J.M. Dent & Sons Ltd., London, p. 489.
3. Ornstein, R., *The Moral Vision of Jacobean Tragedy,* The University of Wisconsin Press Madison, 1960, p. 129.
4. Quoted in Kaufmann, *op. cit.*, p. 231.
5. *Ibid.*, p. 234.
6. Eliot, T.S., *Selected Essays*, New York, 1950, pp. 96-97.
7. Nicoll, A., *British Drama*, Doaba House, New Delhi, p. 110.
8. Ornstein, *op. cit.*, p. 149.
9. *Ibid.*, pp. 149-50.
10. *Ibid.*, p. 150.
11. Ellis-Fermor, U., *The Jacobean Drama*, Methuen, London, 1960, p. 177.

3

A Brief Outline and the Genre

(A) A BRIEF OUTLINE

The Duchess of Malfi is justly thought to be Webster's best play as the ensuring chapters will seek to prove. Of his three major plays, i.e. the plays that he wrote himself, not in collaboration with others, this is the second. It is one of the best Jacobean tragedies.

As the student has seen, very often the dramatists took the stories for their plays from contemporary books of histories, poems, etc. The story of this play has been taken from William Painter's *Palace of Pleasure* a collection of stories. But all the dramatists altered their stories according to their wish and so has Webster. It will be pointed out later in the chapter: he has always changed with the deliberate invention of increasing the dramatic quality.

The beautiful and young Duchess of Malfi, as the play opens, has been widowed. Her two brothers, the Cardinal and Ferdinand, do not want her to marry again. The reason for this is never explained satisfactorily. They tell her that she must not marry again:

Cardinal: ...privately be married
Under the eaves of night—

Ferdinand:

Think it the best voyage
That ever ye made...but observe
Such ways may properly be said
To be executed than celebrated

C.: The marriage night
Is the entrance into some prison

F.: And those joys
Those lustful pleasures are like heavy sleep
Which do fore-run main's mischief

C.: Fare you well
Wisdom begins at the end: remember it.[1]

This becomes an irritating challenge for the Duchess. Quickly she gets married to Antonio, her steward, the best character in the play—steady and honest, loyal and unambitious:

Ambition, madam, is a great man's madness
That is not kept in chains and close-pent rooms,
But in fair lightsome lodgings and is girt
With the wild noise of prattling visitants,
Which make it lunatic beyond all cure.
Conceive not I am so stupid but I aim
Whereto your favours tend: but he's a fool
That, being a-cold, would thrust his hands i' the fire
To warm them.[2]

All the same, she marries him as soon as her brothers have left for Rome.

Ferdinand, before he goes, employs Bosola as a spy to keep an eye on her. Bosola thus is employed only superficially by the Duchess, as her horse-steward. Actually, he is the spy of Ferdinand and reports to him:

F.: I give you that
To live i' the court here, and observe the Duchess.
To note all the particulars of her haviour,
Which suitors to solicit her for marriage,
And which she best affects. She's a young widow:
I would not have her marry again.[3]

The Duchess marries Antonio and in due time is blessed with a child. By ill-luck, this baby's horoscope falls into Bosola's hands. At once he informs Ferdinand of the birth:

B.: Old Castruccio
I'the morning posts to Rome: by him I'll send
A letter that shall make her brother's galls
O'erflow their livers. This was a thrifty way
Though lust do mask in ne'er so strange disguise,
She's oft found witty, but is never wise.[4]

Yet, for some unknown reason, Webster defers the revenge for some years whereas in the original story it comes at once. In Webster's play, the brothers wreak their revenge after the third child is born.

No sooner than the Duchess realizes that the brothers know about the marriage than she sends Antonio to Ancona, a place where she knows he will be safe, with the children. Soon after he goes the Duchess is imprisoned with Bosola set over her as guard. This happens at Loretto. Here during a ceremony with the Cardinal they, the Duchess and Antonio, are banished from Ancona. Now there is no one, and nowhere, that Antonio can turn to for safety.

The Duchess is mentally tortured in various ways. Everything is ordered by Ferdinand. Her fortitude excites Bosola's admiration and reverence. He had been a cynical malcontent. All this changes.

The Duchess is tortured first by being shown wax figures of Antonio and the children to make her believe that they are dead. Then a group of madmen come to her, talking and dancing. This prison scene (IV: ii) has been compared with the heath-scene in *King Lear* by Lamb. She says:

I am not made yet, to my cause of sorrow
The heaven o'er my head seems made of molten brass
The earth of flaming sulphur, yet I am not mad.
I am acquainted with sad misery
As the tann'd galley-slave is with his oar;
Necessity makes me suffer constantly
And custom makes it easy.[5]

After the dance of the madmen, which has become famous as the anti-masque, is finished, Bosola prepares her for death. She is to be strangled, so the executioners bring cords and coffin.

Ferdinand does not allow her the spiritual consolation given by a priest. So Bosola has to act as one. The Duchess is by now a truly noble figure of tragic dignity. She attains high spiritual dignity in spite of all this, by herself. She kneels down before the hired killers saying that the gates of heaven are low, one has to kneel down in order to enter them. Indeed, she has no parallel in spiritual nobility in this scene, except, perhaps, King Lear:

> Pull and pull strongly, for your able strength
> Must pull down heaven' upon me–
> Yet stay; heaven-gates are not so highly arch'd
> As princes' palaces; they that enter there
> Must go upon their kaees (*kneels*).[6]

After killing her the executioners strangle her other children and Cariola. Then Ferdinand comes in and is shown the corpses. On seeing the dead bodies he utters a line that is the best, most famous single line in Webster.

> Cover her face: mine eyes dazzle: she died Young.[7]

His repentance and punishment starts from now. An intemperate person, his penitence too takes an intemperate form. He is stricken by a mental disease known as lycanthropy. In this a man fancies that he is a wolf. In other words, he becomes what he has been all these days—a wolf. The Cardinal is cold-blooded and passionless. He is haunted by the vision of hell and a devil striking with a rake. The world becomes a living hell for him.

Antonio comes to the brothers, seeking reconciliation. He stops at a place on the way where there are many echoes. They convince him that something is wrong, and he reaches Rome when the Cardinal has already poisoned Julia and hidden the body with the help of Bosola. Antonio enters when it is dark. Bosola mistakes him for Ferdinand and kills him.

There is then a scuffle in the darkness in which Bosola kills the Cardinal and Ferdinand who gives him his death-wound. Just before he dies, at the last moment, Ferdinand gets back his sanity. The ending of the play is fully Jacobean, with the stage strewn with corpses. Delio, a chorus character, announces the heirship of the kingdom by the Duchess's son who had escaped because he had been with Delio. The moral of the play is summed up by Delio:

> Integrity of life is fame's best friend
> Which nobly, beyond death, shall crown the end.[8]

(B) THE GENRE OF THE PLAY

The Duchess of Malfi is known as a revenge tragedy but it is only a label. The play goes far beyond it, like *Hamlet* which has the same label. *King Lear* comes rather near it which is a cosmic tragedy. It has been interpreted in many ways, only a few of these will be discussed here. From his own days revenge tragedy is the most common opinion about it so it will be considered the first though it falls woefully short of explaining the tremendous impact of the play.

(i) *The Revenge Tragedy*

Before starting to discuss it, it is necessary to know something about such plays. F.T. Bowers has divided the Tragedy of Blood into four categories and one of them is the Revenge Tragedy. The first such play was *Gorboduc* which began the tradition. It was a translation and had been praised by Sidney. Then came Kyd's *The Spanish Tragedy* which took London by storm. It became the proto-type of such plays. These plays imitated Senecan tragedies which had been extremely popular in Europe as well as in England. These plays have the following features in common:

(1) One motive power impels the action—that of revenge. It has many side-issues which will be explained later when and as necessary. For example, one of them is that the cause for revenge might have taken place before the play began, as in *Hamlet* or in the present time of the play as in *The Duchess*.

(2) Revenge is enjoined as a sacred duty: the idea that it is irreligious ("Revenge is mine, saith the Lord") is a Christian concept naturally not present in Seneca (4 B.C.). It is enjoined as obligatory, and as a duty not to be neglected, upon the avenger as in *Hamlet*.

(3) Supernatural elements are present. It may be present in the ghost of the victim thirsting after reparation and/or omens, as in *Julius Caesar*.

(4) Deeds of cruelty and violence.

(5) A Machiavellian servant ready to do whatever he is told. He is usually known as the malcontent as he is dissatisfied with himself and the world.

(6) The situation is not created by the hero. Circumstances beyond his control force him to be the avenger. So he is in trouble over the ethics of the situation, though not in *The Duchess*.

(7) Often enough the revenger uses the opportunity for revenge provided by the victim himself.

Great presence of mind is required of him. For example the duel between Hamlet and Laertes with poisoned swords is arranged by Claudius and Hamlet makes use of it. As far as this play is concerned, the last two features are not relevant.

Elizabethan revenge tragedies and Jacobean ones are slightly different. *The Duchess* is definitely Jacobean and the most important difference between the two kinds is the concept of morality—whether revenge is right or not. The revenger is torn by the conflict between religion and duty. *Hamlet* is the very archetype of this particular trait.

The revenge tragedy became more and more refined with the progress of the Jacobean Age. This can be seen in the moral attitude developed by Webster. Not without reason had Swinburne declared: "No poet is morally nobler than Webster."

So these are the features of the revenge tragedy. Now it remains to be seen how many of these can be applied to our play.

A revenger, first of all, should have a just cause for his desire for revenge and this is lacking in our play—there is no adequate motive. The brothers wreak their vengeance merely because she has remarried which is not enough to have her killed. A half-hearted motive is given by Ferdinand—her wealth is wanted:

> Only that I must confess I had had a hope
> Had she continu'd widow, to have gain'd
> An infinite mass of treasures by her death.[9]

This is the only time he says it and that also not very convincingly. He has been under the throes of acute but unconscious incestuous love for his sister. But Freudian theory tells us this, not Webster. There is no valid reason for their anger. "Motiveless malignity" best expresses Ferdinand's anger. Jenkins has observed that the play is "that unique thing, a revenge play without a crime".

The second feature of revenge being enjoined as a sacred duty upon the revenger does not apply, for no one has told Ferdinand to kill her.

The third feature of the supernatural is an almost indispensable part of these plays. Webster makes good use of it. There is no very obvious use of it, like ghosts, etc., but the echo-scene is very like a supernatural one. During the scene the Echo says many fearsome things. Towards the end a passage comes:

> Ant.: Echo, I will not talk with thee
> For thou art a dead thing.
>
> Echo: A dead thing.[10]

This is very refined and sophisticated use of the supernatural. Ghosts crying "Revenge" are not to be seen.

The play abounds in deeds of cruelty and violence. For example, there is the torture of the Duchess. There is what has been called the anti-masque of madmen. There are divine beings, gorgeously dressed and songs and dances, in masques. In this one there are madmen in tattered dress, and they sing and dance discordantly, because it is an anti-masque. Before this exhibition the wax figures of Antonio and their son is shown to her. She naturally takes them for real. Then of course there is her death. Without any doubt it is a violent death—death by strangling, but the Duchess's attitude ennobles it into a spiritual height not to be found anywhere else in Jacobean tragedy. There are ten deaths in the play. The murder of Julia is one of the most sensational deaths in Jacobean tragedy. She manages to get the news of the Duchess's murder from the Cardinal and then says she cannot keep it secret. The Cardinal then makes her swear an oath by kissing the Bible. But the cover of the Bible is poisoned and she dies instantly. So a pious act brings horrible death. This is one of the two most ingenious murders to be found in Jacobean drama—all the more horrible as it is committed by a Cardinal.

One of the requirements of a revenge tragedy is the presence of a Machiavellian malcontent as a servant. Bosola fulfils this function. He is "the only court-gall", a notorious malcontent, but he is transformed by the Duchess's nobility. This will be explained in detail in the analysis of his character.

The next (sixth) trait of the revenge tragedy as given above is that the revenger does not create the situation he finds himself in. This condition does not apply here, nor the seventh, as Ferdinand does not have to use any opportunity presented by his victim. He does not do the heinous deed at all but relegates it to Bosola.

As some of the features of the revenge play apply to this play and some do not, it cannot be called an ideal revenge play. It is far too complex.

It should be pointed out that there are two revenge actions here. The first is Ferdinand's revenge—the killing of the Duchess. It is weakly motivated and unjustified. The second is the revenge for her death by Bosola. He, inflamed by the Duchess's cruel death, kills the two brothers. There are two actions in many such play. In *Hamlet*, Hamlet himself is there and Laertes avenges the death of his father and sister, Polonius and Ophelia.

(ii) Reversed Revenge Tragedy

Jenkins thinks that the play is a reversed Revenge tragedy. He holds that Webster has reversed the nature of the revenge tragedy here. It is not the main protagonist who is the revenger. She undergoes and suffers undeserved revenge. It is not that she commits any crime, she is instead the victim. The unjustness of life is most effectively presented by Webster when he reverses the essential features of the revenge tragedy. The view he presents that life is meaningless, cruel and gloomy could not have been more effectively proclaimed in any other way. This is the reason it has been said that *The Duchess* is a "unique thing—a revenge play without a crime."

(iii) Tragicomedy

M.C. Bradbrook as well as J.R. Mulryne, both think that it is tragicomedy in the sense in which this term is applied to modern plays. Such plays have a basic uncertainty about man's position in this world. The author asks himself: is the world ruled by Divine Purpose (Fate) or by a purposeless, senseless Chance? Moreover, Mulryne says that this question is just asked and not answered, in tragi-comedies. The same happens in our play and this is the reason it leaves such a gloomy impression on the reader. The Duchess's death is meaningless, Antonio too is killed by chance and in the scuffle in darkness the others kill each other. It is as if the gods cruelly "kill us for their sport", as Webster himself says. This is what happens in modern tragi-comedies too, like those of Beckett.

In these plays too there is the idea that there are two opposite views of the universe: that Fate or Divine Purpose rules the world. Everything is pre-ordained and whether this Fate is malignant or benevolent is not the question: ours not to reason why. This is the second view, that chance rules the world, an arbitrary, purposeless Fortune. Mankind is, as Bosola says "the stars' tennis balls". The dramatist can adopt any of these views and expound them. The tragi-comic writer is agnostic. He does not adopt either of these nor denies them. The two views are not set in direct opposition mutually. This eminently modern attitude is the one Webster adopts. Moral uncertainty is the very core of his attitude and the play is a tragi-comedy.

(iv) Melodrama

It is the critic James Smith who expounds this idea. But it is not melodrama in the old sense of being a succession of sensational incidents. The meaning is more philosophical. The melodramatic attitude to man is different from the tragic. The tragic man is an essentially divided creature: "passion and reason, self-division's cause". But the melodramatic man is a whole, not torn by doubts. He is supremely sure of himself, of what is right and also what is wrong. So whatever happens to such a hero comes from outside not from within. His difficulties, obstacles, enemies are all external. Three conclusions are possible in such a case (1) conquest of the hero, (2) defeat of the hero, (3) stalemate. Our play is of the second kind, a melodrama of defeat. The Duchess is the innocent victim of senseless cruelty—she just suffers. Her death is the defeat of goodness and innocence in an arbitrary world.

(v) The Domestic Tragedy

This is one of the four types of Elizabethan tragedies. *Arden of Feversham* (1592) and *A Woman Killed with Kindness* (1607) are the two best examples. Such plays concern a family, not a state and is by nature naturalistic. No royal or aristocratic families are there, it concerns ordinary people and records only everyday events of ordinary life of such persons. Allardyce Nicoll calls "a documentary effect", and that it is the pre-cursor of the modern kitchen-sink drama, highly realistic and domestic.

This feature is not important as far as our play goes. Apart from this there are a few other features. A problem of some kind has to be there along with the death. For example, it is the supposed infidelity of Desdemona that is the problem in *Othello*. Such a problem, however, is not presented with violence and sensational incidents. In this the domestic tragedy differs from a revenge one. Also, there are two or more plots, entirely different from each other in such plays. The plots often complement each other. An example will make this clearer. In *Othello* there is the Othello-Desdemona plot and the Cassio-Bianca plot, brought together so as to complement each other. Finally, real-life scenes, not necessarily sordid, are presented here. There are scenes with possibilities of high poetry of much more than conversational mode. The end is tragic and except for that it is like the modern kitchen-sink play.

Like *Othello*, the conventional and generally accepted opinion about *The Duchess* is that it is a domestic tragedy. But if a systematic study is done it will be seen that it has very few features of one. Out of the features given above, only a few are to be found here. First of all, it is not realistic or concerned with ordinary people. The characters are all from the very highest in society. The Duchess is the sovereign ruler over the kingdom of Malfi. The two brothers belong to the same level. Then also there is no problem here that has to be solved, it is just causeless revenge. Two plots are there: the intrigue of the Cardinal and Julia which is not connected with the main plot in any important manner. Again, the situations presented here are not ordinary situations. The events in Act IV for example, take place in a different, a cosmic dimension.

Yet, the play has been looked upon as a domestic tragedy. This is because whatever happens here happens within a family. The Kingdom of Malfi, the outer world, is not affected. The act of needless vengeance, the murder of the Duchess, the death of the two brothers and of Antonio, all happen within a family circle. Julia is not in this family, but she is an unofficial member of it as she is the mistress of the Cardinal. The real outsider is Bosola, yet he is the nearest person to the Duchess, much nearer than her twin, Ferdinand. From this point of view, the play is a domestic tragedy.

(C) WEBSTER'S TRAGIC VISION

Webster's vision of life was an essentially tragic and essentially moral one Not for nothing had T.S. Eliot written in his poem "Whispers of Immortality":

> Webster was much possessed by death
> He saw the skull beneath the skin.[11]

He, however, saw much more than that. Let not the serious student forget Swinburne's highly sensitive sentence: "No poet is morally nobler than Webster."

Webster finds the world a dismal one and the universe sordid, with the gods malignant ones. In all his plays, he says exactly what Shakespeare says in his *King Lear*:

> As flies to wanton boys are we to the gods,
> They kill us for their sport.

This idea is echoed by Bosola in very much the same way in our play:

> We are the stars' tennis—balls, struck and banded
> Which way it please them.[12]

It is a dark mist in which man is lost. Bosola says at the moment of death that the world is but "a deep pit of darkness" and man is fearfully groping about there. Malignant fate is pursuing him, sometimes Fate and sometimes Chance. Sometimes as in our play, it is the gratuitous cruelty of human beings. The one to whom one turns for safety, like a brother or a servant, turns out to be a relentless persecutor against whom there is no defence or succour.

Yet some characters, at times have a glimpse of a ray of light in this darkness. It finds expression in an emphatic manner in one of the prison scenes. The Duchess says she could curse the stars and after a few lines Bosola say to her "Look you, the stars shine still." This may be taken to mean that the stars, i.e. the gods, are benevolent to man. Man may be rebellious enough to curse them, but they still shine on him. Ironically taken, it can also mean that the stars are entirely different to man's misery. They go on shining, man's misery does not matter.

But man is indomitable. In this "dark Satanic Mills" of a world the only positive value lies in his courage and fortitude. He has integrity in the face of temptation and cruelty. Webster finds hope in this and stresses it again and again, particularly in the Duchess. We admire, nay, revere her strength and the inherent nobility of her character. When she says to Bosola's empty chatter: "I am Duchess of Malfi still." Her nobility, her fortitude makes a different man out of Bosola the cynical malcontent. Her endurance is of a phenomenal kind:

> I am not mad yet, to my cause of sorrow:
> The heaven o'er my head seems made of molten brass,
> The earth of flaming sulphur, yet I am not mad.
> I am acquainted with sad misery
> As the tann'd galley-slave is with his oar;
> Necessity makes suffer constantly
> And custom makes it easy.[13]

When, later, she is facing certain and ignominious death she becomes a figure of titanic proportions,—a figure of such tragic dignity that no one can rival. It is a sphere of spiritual nobility where none can follow except King Lear in the prison scene. She kneels down in spiritual humility because heaven's gates are low, proud persons cannot pass under it.

Even excepts this unique example, integrity or nobility in other than a spiritual sense can be found in other characters also, as in Antonio. Bosola also, paradoxically, gives glimpses of it. This is the maxim which is voiced at the end by Delio, the chorus character symbolizing the very spirit of correctness and justice:

> Integrity of life is fame's best friend
> Which nobly, beyond death, shall crown the end.[14]

It has to be pointed out here that Webster's technique of mixing horror with realism heightens the tragic effect. Inga-Stina Ekeblad points out his strategy of mixing stage convention with psychologically true representation. There is the horror-show of the wax effigies and also the Duchess's telling Cariola to give her child "a syrup for his cold". Though this intensifies the tragic effect it is an example of what Ekeblad calls the "impure art" of Webster. It is found in him repeatedly, specially in the two prison scenes. Mixing hornpipes with funerals is but a part of his tragic vision.

References

1. Allen, F. ed. *The Duchess of Malfi: John Webster*, B.I. Pubs., New Delhi, '74, I : i: 15-26, p. 45. All the quotations from the text will be from this edn.
2. I : i : 413-20, p. 49.
3. I : i : 252-57, p. 43.
4. II : iv : 74-79, p. 63.
5. IV : ii : 24-29, p. 100.
6. IV : ii : 234-38, p. 106.
7. IV : ii : 258, p. 108.
8. V : v : 128-29, p. 137.
9. IV : ii : 277-80.
10. V : iv : 40-41.
11. The first two lines of *Whispers of Immortality*, *Collected Poems—1909-1935: T.S. Eliot*. Faber and Faber, London, p. 53.
12. V : iv : 59-60.
13. IV : ii : 24-30.
14. Last two lines of the play.

4

A Scene-wise Analysis

Act I, sc. i

This scene takes place in the presence-chamber of the Duchess. It is a long scene (nearly 500 lines) and many events take place in it. The first part of the scene is like the prologue of the play. Antonio and Delio are present in it. It appears that Antonio had been away from Malfi. He had gone to France to study how they carry on the work of administration in that country. Antonio is an entirely good character with no evil in him, and Delio is a chorus character. The scene begins with a description of the French court. Antonio is full of admiration for it, as it is a court that is morally infallible and seeks to administer justice in the kingdom. His comment is memorable:

> Consider duly that a prince's court
> Is like a common fountain, whence should flow
> Pure silver drops in general, but if 't chance
> Some curs'd example poison 't near the head,
> Death and disease through the whole land spread.[1]

Then the Cardinal and Bosola come in. Even before they enter the stage, we have an evaluation of Bosola by Antonio which is very valuable:

> Here comes Bosola
> The only court-gall; yet I observe the railing
> Is not for simple love of piety
> Indeed he rails at those things which he wants,
> Would be as lecherous, covetous, or proud
> Bloody or envious as any man
> If he had means to be so.[2]

This indeed is a graphic and singularly well-judged picture of Bosola. He is the malcontent who rails at everything, specially at those things which he wants but does not have. Yet this is the one who becomes a positive person at the end, transformed by association with the Duchess. At present he is the conventional malcontent.

It becomes clear from the dialogue between him and the Cardinal that he had, for the latter's sake, served in the galleys for two years. Now he expects to be rewarded. The Cardinal, after asking him whether he wants to be honest, goes out, and we have Bosola's famous evaluation of his and Ferdinand's character:

> He and his brother are like plum-trees that grow crooked over standing-pools: they are rich and o'erladen with fruit; but none but crows, pies and caterpillars feed on them.[3]

After this Castruccio, Silvio, Roderigo and Grisolan enter. All these are chorus characters. Ferdinand also enters and talks to them in a bonhomous manner about sport. Then the cardinal enters, with the Duchess and her maid Cariola and Julia, Castruccio's wife. As the other characters talk Antonio and Delio converse apart and we come to know of the whole-hearted respect of Antonio for the Duchess. He sums it up by saying:

> All her particular worth grows to this sum,—
> She stains the past, lights the times to come.[4]

Then Ferdinand recommends Bosola to the Duchess as the steward of her horses. She gladly accepts. Then, talking apart by themselves Ferdinand tells Bosola that what is actually wants him to do is to spy upon the Duchess. He will ostensibly be the servant of the Duchess, but he is to be a spy. Ferdinand offers him money for this. Bosola's reaction to the proposal and the money is unexpected. Ferdinand gives him gold coins known as angels and he says:

> Take your devils,
> Which hell calls angels: these curs'd gifts would make
> You a corrupter, me an impudent traitor:
> And should I take these, they'd take me to hell.[5]

Herein he is acting like an honest man. He does not mind taking money to kill one, but he draws the line at treachery. It is this streak of honesty that is going to save him in the end.

It is after this that the two brothers caution the Duchess against marriage. Speaking one after the other, they tell her that she must not marry:

> Cardinal: ...privately be married
> Under the eaves of night—
>
> Ferdinand: Think it the best joy
> That e'er ye made....
>
> C.: The marriage night
> Is the entrance into some prison...
> Fare you well.
> Wisdom begins at the end: remember it.[6]

This is a challenge that no mettlesome woman can ignore. It puts the Duchess on her mettle. As soon as the brother leave, she calls for Antonio under the pretext that she wants an account of the expenses incurred during the last few days. He is her steward and keeps the accounts, so it is very reasonable. She takes Cariola into her confidence.

When he comes, she very gradually and artfully leads the conversation in such a way that he comes to understand that she likes him and wants to marry him. It is then that he delivers the famous speech on ambition:

> Ambition madam, is a great man's madness
> That is not kept in chains and close pent rooms,
> But in fair light-some lodgings and is girt
> With the wild notes of prattling visitants.[7]

After this she most charmingly proposes to him:

> Go, go brag
> You have left me heartless; mine is in your bosom
> I hope it will multiply love there...
> Awake, awake man!
> I do here put off all vain ceremony,
> And only do appear to you a young widow

That claims you for her husband, and, like a widow
I use but half a blush in it.[8]

At that time, if a man and a woman took solemn vows in the presence of a witness it was a legally valid marriage. So the two of them take their marriage vows in the presence of Cariola and are legally married. One thing should be pointed out. It is an example of Webster's irony as well as a premonition of evil. The Duchess kisses Antonio and says:

here upon your lips
I sign your *Quietus est.*[9]

This phrase means "it is finished". It is a legal phrase meaning that accounts have been presented and have been found correct. But these were the last words of Christ upon the cross. So, though it is a legal, technical phrase it carries the meaning of death. It is a famous example of Webster's masterly use of irony.

So this is a long scene and a very significant one. It can be divided into several sections.

(1) Up till the entrance of the Cardinal and Bosola is the Prologue.

(2) Then the actual scene starts. Ferdinand talks with the others and the Duchess and the Cardinal enters and Ferdinand gets her to employ Bosola.

(3) Then the two brothers warn the Duchess against marriage.

(4) Then comes the charming proposal scene and the marriage. Thus, it can be easily divided into four sections.

It is a most significant scene as in it are sown the seeds of the later actions. The first Act consists of this one scene only.

Act II, sc. i

This scene is in the nature of a link-scene, bridging the gap between the two important scenes preceding it and following it. Here Bosola gives vent to his misanthropy. He says to Castruccio:

Man stands amaz'd to see his deformity
In any other creature but himself...

And though continually we bear about us
A rotten and dead body, we delight
To hide it in rich tissue.[10]

By this time the Duchess is pregnant with her first child and Bosola suspects it. After some time Antonio and Delio enter and Antonio confides in the latter. After their talk the Duchess enters with her ladies and Bosola gives her some apricots as a present. The Duchess eats them and they make her feel unwell and she withdraws. The scene ends here.

Actually, the apricots have brought on her birth-pains and in the next scene she will give birth to her first child. That is the reason why this scene is a link-scene. In the former scene, she got married and in the next she will bring forth the first child. This scene meanwhile links the two together. Antonio is bewildered, he does not know what to do. Delio gives him some good practical advice about what can be done at this time. They will pretend that Bosola's apricots have brought on this illness. So they will say that the Duchess has been poisoned by Bosola and is to keep to her rooms and everybody else is also confined to his rooms. This is good advice as while everyone is confined to his rooms the Duchess can give birth. Antonio naturally takes this advice.

Thus, though the scene is not important in itself, it acts as a link-scene between two important ones.

Act II, sc. ii

This too is a link-scene as in it the Duchess gives birth to her first baby. Rumour is rife in the palace. Servants gossip and say there has been a French plot to murder the Duchess. Antonio tells everyone that a lot of jewellery is missing. So the gates are to be shut and everyone is to keep to his rooms. Then when Antonio and Delio are alone on the stage Cariola brings the news that the Duchess has given birth to a son. The scene ends here.

Act II, sc. iii

This is a very important scene though a short one as in it the information that a child is born to the Duchess becomes known to Bosola and he sends the news to the two brothers. It begins in the courtyard of the palace at night and Bosola enters with a dark lantern. Antonio also enters.

Antonio is in a very anxious state and he talks to Bosola. He accuses the latter of having poisoned the Duchess and forbids him to leave the palace. But in the darkness and in his flustered state of mind he most carelessly drops a piece of paper and does not notice it. After he goes Bosola picks it up and reads it. This paper is the horoscope of the new-born child. This all-important paper carries in it the information that a male child has been born on such and such a date, in such and such a place. Bosola is overjoyed, though it does not give the name of the father:

> Old Castruccio
> I' the morning posts to Rome: by him I'll send.
> A letter that shall make her brothers' galls
> O'erflow their livers. This was a thrifty way!
> Though lust do make in ne'er so strange disguise,
> She's oft found witty, but is never wise.[11]

This is a scene of only 79 lines but a very important scene. Webster, however, departs from the original story as given by Painter in that he delays the revenge till the birth of the third child.

Act II, sc. iv

In this scene, the intrigue between Julia and the Cardinal is brought in. Julia is Castruccio's wife and the mistress of the Cardinal. This is not long enough to be a sub-plot. It is also clear that the Cardinal is not in love with her any longer. Julia knows, and as soon as he goes out Delio comes in and she starts flirting with him. In the midst of this, a servant comes and says that her husband has come and given a letter to Ferdinand that has sent him out of his mind with anger.

It is a scene of only 75 lines long and serves only to introduce Julia to us. It is not an important one.

Act II, sc. v

Ferdinand after having received the all-important letter from Bosola is nearly mad with anger. He says to the Cardinal in ungoverned rage:

> I have this night digg'd up a mandrake
> And I am grown mad with 't.[12]

A few lines later his overwrought state of mind becomes clear:

Rhubarb, O for rhubarb
To purge this choler! here is the cursed day
To prompt my memory; and here 't shall stick
Till of her bleeding heart I make a sponge
To wipe it out.[13]

He goes on talking still more wildly and the Cardinal all along tries to control him. Ferdinand says:

I could kill her now
In you or in myself; for I do think
It is some sin in us heaven doth revenge
By her.[14]

His violence and intemperance are contrasted with the Cardinal who, though angry is entirely master of himself. His is a cold anger, much more terrible than that of Ferdinand:

Yes but I can be angry
Without this rapture: there is not in nature
A thing that makes man so deform'd, so beastly
As intemperate anger. Change yourself.[15]

This is one of the longest Acts in the play, containing five scenes. Some of the scenes are not very important but all of them are necessary, none of them are redundant or expendable. Some important action or another takes place in them. Webster's scenes, from this point of view are economical, he uses each of them to serve some purpose on other. The most expendable from this point of view would seem to be sc. iv but in this scene, Julia is introduced to us and her relationship with the Cardinal. The scene thus introduces us to the only action that comes near to a sub-plot.

Act III, sc. i

Quite a considerable time has passed between this scene and the last, for the Duchess has given birth to two more children. Why the two brothers have been inactive for these two years is inexplicable. But now they have come here. Antonio tells Delio:

The Lord Ferdinand, that's newly come to court
Doth bear himself right dangerously.[16]

After some more talk in which it becomes clear that there is talk about corruption in the Court, Ferdinand comes, tells the Duchess that he has arranged for a marriage between her and Count Malatesti. The Duchess objects and he hypocritically reassures her that he believes in her innocence. Everyone except he goes out. Then Bosola comes and it is clear that as yet they do not know who the husband of the Duchess is. Ferdinand has made Bosola get a duplicate key to her bedroom. The scene ends here.

This is a small one (93 lines only) and a minor one. But though short it serves several purposes:

(1) two more children are born to the Duchess.

(2) Ferdinand arranges her marriage with Malatesti.

(3) He obtains a duplicate key to her room.

This is typical of Webster: that in a short scene where no important events take place, he yet does three important things. It fills us with dread and premonitions of evil—what is Ferdinand going to do?

Act III, sc. ii

This scene takes place in the bedroom of the Duchess. It is an entirely domestic scene between husband and wife and maid. The Duchess says that this night she wants to be alone. Antonio then jokes about the misfortunes of a single life and gives three examples from classical myths of how those who wanted to remain single were punished by the gods. Daphne became a laurel tree. Syrinx became a hollow reed and Anaxarete became marble. Then she talks to them, not looking at them and both of them go quickly away without telling her while she is still talking.

Now Ferdinand comes. She still goes on talking without knowing this. She ends her speech thus:

> For knowing whether I am doom'd to live or die,
> I can do both like a prince.[17]

Then he suddenly confronts her and gives her a poniard. He gives vent to great anger and indignation at her immorality and does not listen to anything she says. Finally goaded beyond endurance she says that she is married. He is a long railing speech upbraids her and ends by saying:

> Let not the sun
> Shine on him till he's dead; let dogs and monkeys
> Only converse with him, and such dumb things
> To which nature denies use to sound his name.[18]

Justly angered, the Duchess asks:

> Why might I not marry?
> I have not gone about in this to create
> Any new world or custom.[19]

There is no valid answer to this, so he only blames her all the more. He delivers a long sermonising speech on reputation in the manner of an allegory. She asks:

> Why should only I
> of all the other princes of the world,
> Be cas'd up, like a holy relic? I have youth
> And a little beauty.[20]

Then he goes out and Antonio and Cariola come in. This means that Ferdinand does not see Antonio and does not know that he is her husband.

All three, the Duchess, Antonio and Cariola are frightened and surprised and the Duchess shows the poniard. While they are talking about it there is knocking and Bosola enters and tells them that Ferdinand has gone to Rome, in the middle of the night. The Duchess, quick-witted as she is, quickly fabricates a story about how Antonio has cheated her, and Ferdinand is angry because of it. She tells him to get all the officers of the palace. He goes and she tells Antonio:

> The place you must fly to is Ancona:
> Hire a house there; I will send after you
> My treasure and my jewels. Our weak safety....
> I must now accuse you
> Of such a feigned crime.[21]

Then Bosola comes in and all the officers. She tells them that Antonio has cheated her, confiscates his property and banishes him. He goes out, and after some time the officers also go and Bosola in a speech pretends to sympathise with Antonio. He praises him so much that the Duchess, trusting him, tells him the truth:

> This good man that you speak of is my husband
> I have had three children by him.[22]

She entrusts him with all her treasures and jewellery and tells him to go to Ancona. Bosola advises her to undertake a pilgrimage to Loretto, very near Ancona. The Duchess welcomes the suggestion and goes out, leaving him alone to express his mind:

> What rests but I reveal
> All to my lord?...
> Now for this act I am certain to be raised
> And men that paint weeds to the life are praised.[23]

The scene ends here. It is a scene crowded with events, all leading swiftly to the tragic doom. It is a long scene (323 lines), and the following things happen in it:

(1) Ferdinand comes, giving the Duchess a poniard

(2) She pretends to accuse Antonio of fraud and banishes him.

(3) Bosola praises him and is rewarded with the confession of the Duchess.

This Act is the central Act of the play and this is the most important scene in it. Ironically, the Duchess thinks she is safe but the audience knows it is the opposite. This is an example of Webster's use of dramatic irony.

Act III, sc. iii

This is one of the two middle scenes of the play. In this scene, we are in Rome in the palace of the Cardinal, in the Arragonian brothers' own ground. Most of the male characters in the play are present, except of course, Antonio. It appears from their talk that there is going to be a war in which all of them are to take part, even the Cardinal, for the emperor has come to know of his capacity as a warrior and wants him to join. They talk about the war for some time and then Bosola enters. The other characters talk about him for quite some time. Indeed, the scene is remarkable as these exalted persons talk about an inferior person like him at all. The remarks made by them are significant reflections on his character. The two brothers talk to Bosola in the meantime. He tells them that Antonio is her husband and the Cardinal at once decides to banish them from Ancona, which is a place that is loyal to the Duchess and where she had decided to seek refuge from her brothers. Banished from Ancona she will be at the mercy of Ferdinand. The scene ends with some venomous words from him.

From the point of view of action there is nothing that really takes place in this scene but all the same Webster in his own fashion makes this minor scene serve several purposes:

(1) The Cardinal is to join the war as a warrior.

(2) Bosola tells them that Antonio is the husband of the Duchess.

(3) The Duchess is to be banished from Ancona.

The ceremony of the Cardinal's investiture as a soldier will take place at Loretto. This is the place where the Duchess had thought of going on a pilgrimage.

Some of the significant lines in the scene consist of Ferdinand's venomous spitting:

> Methinks her fault and beauty
> Blend together like leprosy.
> The whiter, the fouler I make it a question
> Whether her beggar brats are ever christened.[24]

The lines on Bosola emphasize his scholarliness in out-of-the-way things like the colour of Achilles's beard or the nature of Hercules's club. It is not clear whether they are meant seriously or not. Perhaps those remarks are made facetiously, but the very fact that these exalted persons at all talk about him is significant.

This scene, thus though a minor one, Webster in his own manner makes serve as enumerated above. He is a very economical writer when it serves his purposes.

Act III, sc. iv

We have passed the mid-point of the play. This scene takes place at the shrine of Our Lady of Loretto. Here the Cardinal is invested as a warrior. It is more like a masque than an ordinary scene, with songs and dumb-shows.

At first two pilgrims enter. They inform the audience that the Cardinal is to give up his post as a cardinal and be invested as a warrior. They also tell us that the Duchess has come as a pilgrim. Then there is a dumb show. In this dumb show, the Cardinal delivers his cross, his hat which is the special hat worn by Cardinals and ring at the shrine and is given a sword, helmet and shield and spurs. Then Antonio comes with the Duchess and the children. They are all banished by the Cardinal and persons representing the State of Ancona.

During this entire ceremony a song is sung to solemn music by churchmen, the first four lines being quoted below:

> Arms and honours deck thy story,
> To thy fame's eternal glory!
> Adverse fortune ever fly thee;
> No disastrous fate come near thee.[25]

This song has 22 lines, all exalting the Cardinal. After the song all except the two pilgrims who had been there in the beginning go out and the two of them talk. They are puzzled that the Duchess has been banished. Their sympathies are with her and Antonio and they rightly guess that the vengeful brothers are at the base of it. Ferdinand had taken the wedding-ring of the Duchess and had vowed he would take his revenge. The first pilgrim voices the opinion of the people.

> Alas Antonio!
> If that a man be thrown into a well,
> No matter who sets hand to 't, his own weight
> Will bring him sooner to the bottom.[26]

This is an important scene from the point of view of action, though not from that of speech. Three actions take place here, all in dumb show:

(1) The Cardinal gives up his cardinalhood.

(2) He is invested as a warrior.

(3) The Duchess, with family, is banished.

All these are in dumb-show, which means that the whole thing is like a masque. This impression is strengthened by the solemn song that accompanies the whole show.

This scene is easily divided into three parts:

(1) The first part consists of the dialogue between the two pilgrims.

(2) The middle part is the dumb show.

(3) The rest of the scene.

So, the balance of the scene is not quite perfect, the third part is much longer than the first.

The masque or the dumb show is extraordinary in that it is not exactly like a masque. Music is there, but it is solemn music sung by "churchmen" and the action is not a merry or beautiful one as it always is in masques. From the point of view of the play it is an entirely negative one as the Duchess is banished and threatened. Up till now her case had seemed to be hopeful but now we realise that tragic doom is hastening upon them. Allardyce Nicoll says:

> Webster's was a peculiar half-genius. In some respects he exhibits the true dramatist's skill in the handling of the scene and hardly any could match him in the conjuring of macabre situations illuminated by a poetic imagination ever dwelling on the thought of death.[27]

This is actually the point of no return for the Duchess and for the play. Her days of happiness are over. After this there is only helpless agony in store for her. Now Webster's tragic vision will gradually and fully unfurl itself. This scene is thus a crucial one. Yet the surprising thing is that there is no dialogue to speak of in this scene. All the dialogue there is, is between the two pilgrims who have nothing to do with the actual play. Webster's matchless poetry, his irony, his wonderful imagery,—none of these are to be seen in this scene. Webster's art surpasses the art and artifice of Jacobean drama here, for, without using any speeches at all he has made this scene so effective—merely by keeping silence. Everything is done by the dumb show which is hardly a proper masque. H.T. Price calls this a "figure in action". The point will be explained in the discussion of his imagery. Such a masterly use of an entirely conventional mode can hardly be seen in Jacobean drama. After this we will read his eloquent poetry but here by using an artificial stage convention like the dumb show he shows himself to be a master of stagecraft as well as a dramatist. This is one of the middle scenes of the play.

Act III, sc. v

From this scene starts the torture of the Duchess. This is the first such scene. At first the Duchess is with Antonio, her children and a few loyal followers who are determined not to desert her whatever happens. She has had a dream which is a premonition of the evil days to come:

> Methought I wore my coronet of state
> And on a sudden all the diamonds
> Were chang'd to pearls.[28]

Just as diamonds stand for prosperity so do pearls stand for tears. Antonio has no difficulty in understanding her dream:

> My interpretation
> Is, you will weep shortly; for to me the pearls
> Do signify your tears.[29]

Then Bosola comes with a letter from Ferdinand. He wants to see Antonio and he words it most ambiguously which the Duchess has no difficulty in understanding:

> Send Antonio to me; I want his head in a business.[30]

"Head" means both his brains, his advice and also the actual head. It is at once understood by the Duchess:

> A politic equivocation!
> He doth not want your counsel but your head.[31]

She tells him to take refuge in Milan with their eldest child and they bid farewell to each other, never to meet again. After they have gone comes one of the most famous lines in Jaco bean drama. The Duchess says:

> My laurel is all wither'd.[32]

The only other such a half-line is to be found in Shakespeare but the two cannot really be compared as the latter is expressive of positive values. It is in *King Lear*, said by Edgar: "Ripeness is all." But the two should not be compared as Webster's is negative and Shakespeare's positive.

After this Bosola, his face in a mask, comes with a guard. He is to keep the Duchess a prisoner. There is a long dialogue between them. He takes her to her palace and tells her she will never see her husband and tries to dissuade her from loving Antonio by maligning him.

As a scene, it is quite a long one, having 142 lines. It is clearly divisible into two nearly equal parts, the first consisting of 90 lines when Antonio starts for Milan with the eldest child and the second starts with Bosola's entrance as her prison guard. From this scene onwards her language and attitude changes. Referring to the usual reference to death and decay in Jacobean tragedy Walter Allen says:

> In *The Duchess of Malfi* even that old-fashioned element is spiritualised by being made expressive of the Duchess's self-conscious glorying in sorrow.[33]

The last line of the scene may be as an example of this:

> I am arm'd 'gainst this misery;
> Bent to all sway of the oppressor's will:
> There is no deep valley but near some great hill.[34]

This last is a couplet in the manner of Senecan "sentences" which will be commented upon when the versification is being discussed later.

Act IV, sc. i

This is the famous prison-scene which is compared often with *King Lear*. It has been endlessly commented upon by everyone who has written on him. A few representative comments are given below:

(1) As they [the Duchess's sufferings'] are not like inflictions *of this life* so her language seems *not of this world*.... She speaks the dialect of despair. To move a horror skillfully, to touch a soul to the quick...this only a Webster can do.[35]

(2) Only the greatest of the world's dramatists have succeeded in making physical violence subserve the ends of dramatic atmosphere.... His finest use of physical

horror is undoubtedly to be found in the fourth Act of *The Duchess of Malfi.*[36]

(3) Rage, anguish, harrowing fear, heart-crazing crime.
Make monstrous all the murderous face of Time.
Shown in the spheral orbit of a glass.[37]

(4) In these scenes Webster gathers together the streams of thought and purpose, bringing up to the surface undercurrents of actions and relations hitherto unknown to the characters themselves.[38]

(5) It is this structural counterpoint of "convention" and "realism" this concentrated "impurity" of art, that gives the scene its peculiar nature; indeed it contains the meaning of the scene.[39]

Only five opinions have been given here, as representing the critical views. There are many others that are not given for lack of space. Now let us look at the scene itself.

The scene opens with a dialogue between Ferdinand and Bosola. He asks Bosola how the Duchess is and Bosola's answer is very significant, more as to the change that he has undergone than as a comment on the Duchess: In a speech of eight lines he uses the word "noble" twice:

...a behavior so noble
As gives a majesty to adversity.[40]

It is a triumph for the Duchess as well as for Webster's art of characterisation that Bosola, the Machiavellian, the "court-gall" changes as he does in the play. From a cynic he becomes a normal man. When Ferdinand goes out and the Duchess enters Bosola's greeting to her is eloquent of his sympathy for he says: "All comfort to your grace." He gives her Ferdinand's message that as he had vowed never to see her again, so in order to keep that vow he has come to the palace and will meet her in darkness for reconciliation with her.

He comes and after talking insultingly to her, pretends to give her his hand to kiss. Actually, it is a dead man's hand. By the time she realizes it, he is gone. His method of torturing her is not at an end as after the lights are brought the wax figures of

Antonio and the children are shown to her. She is not allowed to come near the figures or to touch them as she will then realize that they are artificial. She is in despair and talks of fasting to death. She says: "I could curse the stars". Then Bosola says the extremely significant half-line:

> Look you, the stars shine still.[41]

This can be interpreted in a positive as well as negative manner, as has already been pointed out. Positively, it means that the stars (gods) are benevolent; though mankind may rebel they will still give light, and the negative meaning is that they are totally indifferent to man. They will go on shining, without caring for man's agony and pain. Emphasizing the negative meaning, H.T. Price says:

> He points to the stars, indifferent to her curses, pitiless, terrible—surely this line is among the greatest ever written.[42]

Had this critic pointed out the two ways in which the line can be seen, his claim that it is among the greatest lines ever written would have been much stronger.

She leaves and Ferdinand enters. He is overjoyed at the torture he is inflicting on her. Bosola asks him why he is doing this and asks him to end it all. He, paying no attention to Bosola plans the next torture: to bring all the madmen from the madhouse and introduce them to her. Bosola cannot endure it and says that when he sees her next it will be to comfort her.

Act IV, sc. ii

This is the scene in which the murder of the Duchess takes place. But before that happens, she is subjected to further torture. Madmen are brought in, no madder than Ferdinand himself who had become a pathological case long ago. The scene contains some of the best poetic passages in Webster. Cariola says to the Duchess that she will live to shake this misery off and the latter says:

> Thou art a fool:
> The robin-red-breast and the nightingale
> Never live long in cages.[43]

Then come some of the most famous lines in Webster:

I'll tell thee a miracle;
I am not mad yet, to my cause of sorrow:
The heaven o'er my head seems made of molten brass
The earth of flaming sulphur, yet I am not mad.
I am acquainted with sad misery
As the tann'd galley-slave is with his oar;
Necessity makes me suffer constantly,
And custom makes it easy.[44]

Then the madmen come in. Here we have what is an anti-masque: (1) whereas in masques supernatural characters are used, we have subnormal men. (2) Gorgeous costumes are used in masques and here the men are dressed in tattered clothes. (3) Beautiful songs accompanied by harmonious music are used in masques and here we have a doggerel is sung to "a dismal kind of music". (4) The setting in a masque is gorgeous and here the setting is the room in which the Duchess is imprisoned. So, from every point of view it is an anti-masque.

The mad men talk among themselves and sing and dance, and then go out. Then Bosola, disguised as an old man, enters. He speaks in prose. He had said that when he next saw her it will be to comfort her, and he does his best to comfort her now. Ferdinand had denied her even the basic right of meeting a priest before killing her. So now Bosola the cynic, the Machiavellian takes on the office of a spiritual comforter, a priest:

> Didst thou ever see a lark in a cage? Such is the soul in the body: this world is like her little turf of grass, and the heaven o'er our heads like her looking-glass, only gives us a miserable knowledge of the small compass of our prison.[45]

After some more talk the executioners enter with a coffin, cords and a bell, signifying that she is to die by strangling. Then, as Bosola has taken on, willy-nilly, the function of a priest he chants some couplets. He is not a priest so he cannot chant in Latin, but he does his best:

Strew your hair with powder sweet
Den clean linen, bathe your feet,
And (the foul fiend more to check)

A crucifix let bless your neck:
'Tis now full tide 'tween night and day
End your groan and come away.[46]

It is actually much longer, only the closing lines have been given here. Some of the most pathetic lines come here when the Duchess tells Cariola to give the child some syrup for his cold.

When Bosola asks her if she is afraid of death by strangling, she says:

What would it please me to have my throat cut
With diamonds? Or to be smothered
With cassia or to be shot to death with pearls?
I knew death has ten thousand doors
For men to take their exit.[47]

Then preparing for death there are the unparalleled lines in Jacobean literature or indeed literature of any period. Not even *King Lear* can come near it, for Lear has Cordelia when he talks of singing like larks in a cage, but the Duchess has nobody. Her lines have a spiritual nobility unequalled in literature. She is prepared, not for death, but for entering heaven:

Pull and pull strongly, for your able strength
Must pull down heaven upon me—
Yet stay; heaven-gates are not so highly arch'd
As princes' palaces; they that enter there
Must go upon their knees. (*kneels*)[48]

After killing her the executioners kill the children and Cariola.

Then Ferdinand enters. The first thing he says is to ask: "Is she dead?" He is absolutely bubbling with joy. This does not change when he sees the dead bodies of the children. Then he sees her face. At once a palpable change comes over him and we have the famous line:

Cover her face: mine eyes dazzle: she died young.[49]

This one and single line is so effective that it has been endlessly commented upon. It shows Webster's art at its best. Nowhere is the saying that art lies in concealing art better exemplified than in this line. It is not a full line of magniloquent poetry. On the other hand, it is a line of broken phrases. Now indeed Ferdinand's retribution starts. He has lost the power of coherent speaking. His repentance that is searing in its intensity starts now. In the first onslaught of it all he can think of is to blame Bosola for carrying out his directions and not sparing her. He has the effrontery to ask Bosola by whose authority he has killed her and when Bosola says "By yours" he lashes out:

> Mine! was I her judge?
> Did any ceremonial form of law
> Doom her to not-being?[50]

A few lines later we are given the first premonition of his future madness:

> The wolf shall find her grave, and scrape it up
> Not to devour the corpse, but to discover
> The horrid murder.[51]

After more of mutual recrimination he makes his exit on a most significant line: one that definitely foretells his madness:

> I will go hunt the badger by owl-light
> 'Tis a deed of darkness.[52]

Bosola then quickly takes off his mask and tries to revive the Duchess. She gains consciousness for a brief time and utters just two words : "Antonio" and "Mercy" and dies. Now Bosola has changed utterly. He vows to avenge her death by killing the Cardinal and Ferdinand. He is on the side of justice and pity now. As has already been remarked the change in him is an example of Webster's mastery in the art of characterization. It is the nobility of the Duchess that has changed him.

No praise can be extravagant for these two scenes. Some representative remarks have already been given in the analysis of the first prison scene. Usually the two are considered together. Looking at this scene, in particular, it is a long scene (370 lines). It is the second scene in the play and can be divided into no less than five parts:

(1) Up till line 60, till the entrance of the mad.

(2) The anti-masque of the madmen.

(3) Exit of the madmen and entrance of Bosola. Her murder and that of Cariola and the children.

(4) Entrance of Ferdinand and his exit in line 330.

(5) Bosola's attempt to revive her and his vow to avenge her.

All the five divisions are well-enough demarcated and the anti-masque has already been commented upon above. It is true that no praise is enough for this scene, yet there are a few points of criticism that have been raised against it. Webster has been accused of departure from realism for the sake of dramatic effect. Even after being strangled and taken for dead the Duchess recovers enough to speak two words. Had it been any other kind of death it would have been excusable but in death by strangling the first organs to be affected are the vocal cords. Such a victim cannot speak and here the Duchess speaks, be it only two words.

Against this criticism it can be said that the same thing happens to Desdemona. She has been strangled to death by Othello and yet she recovers consciousness for long enough to exonerate him from the murder and take the blame on herself. So Webster has here followed an example set by no less a dramatist than Shakespeare himself.

The third or the middle part of the scene is the most important and the longest. The two preceding and the two following are short. So, Webster has tried to balance the parts by putting the longest and the most important in the middle. It is stagecraft-wise, a well-balanced scene.

But all these remarks seem to be entirely unnecessary when the tremendous impact of the scene is considered. As has already been pointed out, this scene has a spiritual grandeur unequalled in drama of all time.

Act V, sc. i

This is a link-scene in which Antonio and Delio are in the public square of Milan. Then Pescara and Julia enter to talk to them with the Cardinal's letter to give Antonio's property to them. Antonio understands the motive behind this move only too well and Delio promises to support him. This scene merely links the foregoing and the next scene together.

Act V, sc. ii

This is the scene in which Ferdinand's madness is diagnosed. Pescara is talking to the doctor who is treating him and the doctor tells him that Ferdinand is suffering from lycanthropy in which the patient believes that he is a wolf. Ferdinand enters and he does behave like a mad man, falling upon his shadow and trying to throttle it. The Cardinal tries to find excuses for him but they are feeble ones. When everyone goes out and he is left alone with Bosola he pretends not to know about the Duchess's death. The Cardinal tells him that Antonio is in Milan and that he should seek him out and kill him. When the Cardinal leaves him alone on the stage Julia comes. She is attracted to Bosola and flirts with him. Bosola responds in kind and asks her to find out why the Cardinal is out of spirits. After some more badinage he goes out and the Cardinal enters. Julia pleads with him to tell her why he is gloomy and irritable and the Cardinal tries to put her off. Julia insists and finally the Cardinal confides in her. Terrified, she says that she cannot keep this secret and he then swears her to secrecy by making her kiss the Bible. Here occurs one of the most sensational deaths in Jacobean drama for he has poisoned the cover of the Bible:

> ...thou'rt poisoned with that book
> ...I knew that thou couldst not keep thy counsel
> I have bound thee to 't by death.[53]

This is one of the most renowned deaths in Jacobean drama as it is a Cardinal who kills by poisoning the Bible. A pious act is used for murder and that too by a Cardinal. It is sacrilege as well as a crime. The audience will be stunned at the villainy of the Cardinal. This, more than anything else, highlights his villainy.

Bosola enters before she dies. The Cardinal binds him to secrecy and threatens him with dire consequences. He makes Bosola promise to kill Antonio and to come to him at midnight to hide the dead body. After he leaves Bosola says he will seek out Antonio to warn and save him and also to avenge the murder of the Duchess. He is truly penitent, there is no hypocrisy in him:

> O Penitence, let me truly taste thy cup,
> That throws men down only to raise them up.[54]

Act V, sc. iii

This is the famous scene known as the echo-scene. In it Webster makes use of supernatural elements which are a must in revenge tragedy. The supernatural means he uses however are not ghosts or portents. It is much subtler than that, so much so that it can hardly be called supernatural. It is, rather, a natural phenomenon used in such a way as to suggest the supernatural. Hereby, again, Webster is master of stagecraft and subtle. Nothing so crude for him as a Ghost crying "Revenge"!

There is a fortification where Antonio and Delio have come and as the place is in ruins it gives forth echoes. All these echoes are truly echoing, i.e., a repetition of the last words of the actors. Yet they are such that they fill their minds with fear and premonitions of evil. These echoes are:

(1) Like death that we have
(2) Deadly accents
(3) A thing of sorrow
(4) That suits it best
(5) Ay, wife's voice
(6) Do not
(7) Be mindful of thy safety
(8) O, fly your fate
(9) Thou art a dead thing
(10) Never see her more.[55]

Considerable artistry is needed to arrange the dialogue in such a way as to produce these echoes, but Webster's art is more than equal to the challenge. The scene shows how a perfectly natural phenomenon is used to serve a contemporary convention, that of the use of the supernatural element in revenge tragedy.

Act V, sc. iv

This is the last but one scene of the play and the death of the principal characters will occur one by one. It takes place in the palace of the Cardinal and Ferdinand, and chorus characters like Pescara, Malatesti and others are present along with the Cardinal. The latter tells the others that he will withdraw now and tells them not to come if they hear any noise or cries for help. After they go the Cardinal makes his intentions clear. He wants to convey Julia's corpse to her own home and wants privacy for it. Then he goes out and Bosola whom he had called at midnight to do this work comes in. At the same time Ferdinand comes and utters a famous line:

> Strangling is a very quiet death.[55]

Once can imagine him almost whispering it and the spectators are spell-bound. Hearing it Bosola sees that he must be cautious as he is giving voice to the guilty secret. Then Antonio enters. It is dark and, in the darkness, Bosola takes him for Ferdinand and gives him his death-wound in all innocence. He kills by mistake the one man he would have liked to save before all others. It is here that he expresses Webster's tragic vision in the famous lines:

> We are the stars' tennis-balls, struck and banded
> which way please them.[57]

This is the darkest vision of man's fate given by Webster: man being pursued by an actively malignant fate as has been explained in the section dealing with Webster's tragic vision. Now more than ever Bosola is determined on avenging the death of Antonio and others.

Act V, sc. v

Now for the first time we see the Cardinal's retribution overtaking him. The world has become a living hell for him for he sees the devil striking at him:

> When I look into the fish-pond in my garden
> Methinks I see a thing arm'd with a rake
> That seems to strike at me.[58]

It is a devil who carries a rake with which he strikes at sinners. The Cardinal is at last feeling terror and guilt.

Then Bosola enters, bringing Antonio's body. Bosola, determined to kill him, attacks him. But the Cardinal has already told Pescara and the others not to come even if they hear any noise. So, they all (four of them), appear above on the a balcony and though the Cardinal cries for help they do not come at first. Then they think that something is really wrong and come down to find out what the matter is. But in the meantime, Bosola stabs the Cardinal repeatedly. In the confusion Ferdinand enters, thinking that some battle is going on. He too wounds the Cardinal (he is mad after all, and it is dark), and gives Bosola his death-wound and Bosola kill him. At the last moment he gets his sanity back.

> My sister, O my sister,! there is the cause on't
> Whether we fall by ambition, blood or lust,
> Like diamonds, we are cut with our own dust.

Bosola is still living when Pescara and the others enter. He explains the whole thing to them; how the Duchess has been avenged and all the others died. Before his death he utters one of the gloomiest passages in Webster:

> O this gloomy world!
> In what a shadow or deep pit of darkness,
> Doth womanish and fearful mankind live!
> Let worthy minds ne'er stagger in distrust
> To suffer death or shame for what is just:
> Mine is another voyage.[60]

Now the stage is strewn with corpses in the most traditional manner of revenge tragedies and the time has come for the restitution of moral order. This is done by Delio who enters with Antonio's son. He makes it clear that this boy will inherit the kingdom and ends the play by uttering a Senecan couplet that sums up the moral lesson Webster wants to convey:

> Integrity of life is fame's best friend
> Which nobly, beyond death, shall crown the end.[61]

So the play ends like a Jacobean revenge tragedy with five deaths in this last scene and there are more deaths that have gone before, like those of Antonio and Julia. Bosola's last words, famous as they are, again give his tragic vision of the world: of mankind pursued by dark and malignant fate. He also makes it clear that for people like Bosola the end remains ambiguous: "Mine is another voyage."

References

1. I : i : 11-15, p. 35.
2. I : i : 23-28, p. 36.

3. I : i : 50-53, p. 36.
4. I : i : 214-15, p. 41.
5. I : i : 264-67, p. 43.
6. I : i : 313-25, p. 45.
7. I : i : 413-16, p. 49.
8. I : i : 441-52, pp. 49-51.
9. I : i : 456-57, p. 50.
10. II : i : 56-64, p. 53.
11. II : ii : 74-79, p. 63.
12. II : v : 1-2, p. 67.
13. II : v : 12-16, p. 67.
14. I : v : 61-64, p. 69.
15. II : v : 53-69, p. 69.
16. III : i : 18-19, p. 70.
17. III : ii : 59-60, p. 75.
18. III : ii : 92-95, p. 76.
19. III : ii : 98-100, p. 76.
20. III : ii : 127-30, p. 77.
21. III : ii : 164-69, p. 79.
22. III : ii : 67 & 72, p. 82.
23. III : ii : 318-23, p. 84.
24. III : iii : 61-64, p. 86.
25. III : iv : 7-10, p. 87.
26. III : iv : 38-41, p. 88.
27. A. Nicoll, *op. cit.*, p. 110.
28. III : v : 13-15, p. 89.
29. *Ibid.*
30. III : v : 27, p. 90.
31. III : v : 28-30, p. 90.
32. III : v : 91, p. 92.
33. Allen, *op. cit.*, pp. 27-28.
34. III : v : 141-42, p. 93.
35. Allen, *op. cit.*, p. 11.
36. *Ibid.*, p. 10.
37. *Ibid.*, Frontispiece.

38. Ellis-Fermor, U., *op. cit.*, p. 190.
39. Kaufmann, *op. cit.*, p. 252.
40. IV : i : 5-6, p. 94.
41. IV : i : 98, p. 97.
42. Kaufmann, *op. cit.*, p. 246.
43. IV : ii : 12-14, p. 100.
44. IV : ii : 23-30, p. 100.
45. V : ii : 123-29, p. 103.
46. V : ii : 184-89, p. 105.
47. IV : ii : 210-14, p. 106.
48. IV : ii : 224-28, p. 106.
49. IV : ii : 258, p. 108.
50. IV : ii : 294-96, p. 109.
51. IV : ii : 304-06, p. 109.
52. IV : ii : 329-30, p. 111.
53. V : ii : 278-80, p. 124.
54. V : ii : 348-49, p. 126.
55. V : iii, Lines 19, 22, 25-27, 30, 33, 37, 41-42, pp. 127-28.
56. V : iv : 35, p. 130.
57. V : iv : 59-60, p. 131.
58. V : v : 5-7, p. 132.
59. V : v : 79-81, p. 135.
60. V : v : 108-13, p. 137.
61. V : v : 128-29, p. 137.

5
The Major Themes

Unity of theme is a must for a literary work to give it a good structure. For example, the great Indian work *Kathasaritsagara* is denied the dignity of an epic as it lacks unity of theme. However, flabby or haphazard the structure of a play might be but if the central theme is firmly and convincingly given then the entire work is a successful whole. The theme, as such, is the most important part of a work. A literary work need not be limited to just one theme. It might have several sub-themes in addition to a central theme. Shakespeare's plays for that matter, have many such. In addition to this, a work can be interpreted in many different ways thematically, as has happened with our play. Different critics have emphasized different themes in it and have interpreted it in their own way. Some of these, though not all, will be discussed now.

(1) The Theme of Revenge

It can never be denied that revenge is the main theme of this play, however unjustifiable the label might be. The fact, that it is unjustified, will become clear as one by one the other themes are discussed. In the discussion on Genre in chapter 3, the topic has already been extensively discussed, so the features, etc. of revenge tragedies are not being mentioned here. The theme of revenge is already introduced and hinted at in the very first scene itself. In this scene when the two brothers warn the Duchess against marriage it is mentioned:

> Cardinal: Privately be married under the eaves of night—
>
> Ferdinand: Think't the best voyage
> That e'er you made....

....

C.: The marriage night
Is the entrance into some prison

F.: and those joys
Those lustful pleasures, are like heavy sleep
which do forerun man's mischief.[1]

That is to say, they threaten her with imprisonment and death if she re-marries. This will be done in revenge for disobeying their order. So, it is a case of personal revenge.

Later, in the violence of Ferdinand's reaction to the information that she has got children the theme of personal revenge becomes even clearer. He even uses the word "revenge" (though in a different way) with reference to her:

for I do think
It is some sin in us heaven doth revenge
By her.[2]

He uses the work in relation to "heaven" but it is clear that it is he himself screaming for personal revenge. It is because his own incestuous, sinful and unrecognized love for the Duchess that has prompted it.

(2) The Theme of Reversed Revenge

This is the opposite of the theme of Revenge. This theory takes it for granted that there is no just cause for revenge and this is the view held by Jenkins. Actually speaking there is no just cause for the vengeance wreaked by the two Arragonian brothers. After all, the only offence the Duchess commits is to marry beneath her status. But it is a legally-valid marriage and she had every right to marry. As, goaded beyond endurance, she says:

Why might I not marry?
I have not gone about in this to create
Any new world or customs.[3]

There is no answer to this as Ferdinand knows quite well. So he just goes on reviling her all the more, threatening her and sermonising her. Again a few lines later, she asks:

> Why should only I
> Of all the other princes of this world
> Be cas'd up like a holy relic? I have youth
> And a little beauty.[4]

Again he does not give her any answer as there is no answer to give. Actually, besides his possessiveness and jealousy and unacknowledged incestuous love there is no reason. So the play remains a paradox, an anomaly—a revenge play without any crime. It is modelled after revenge plays, so it is one. But such a play has to have a crime to justify the theme of revenge. Hamlet's father's ghost comes to Hamlet and enjoins revenge upon him as a sacred duty. So Hamlet has to avenge his father's murder however much it might go against religion. Christianity says "Revenge is mine, Saith the Lord", but for Hamlet it is a duty. In every revenge play, it is the same, but not as far as this one is concerned. This is a revenge play in which no crime has been committed. It is the very reverse of such a tragedy. So Jenkins argues that the theme here is of the reversal of revenge. M.C. Bradbrook is of the same opinion:

> the Duchess is not a criminal and there is no reason why she should be thought of as suffering the tortures of the damned.[5]

(3) A Tragi-Comic Theme

This is the view held by J.R. Mulryne and M.C. Bradbrook: that the theme is typical of tragicomedies. It must be understood that here both of these critics regard tragicomedies not in the way the Elizabethans understood it, but in the modern way. In Elizabethan times, the tragicomedy as developed mainly by Beaumont and Fletcher meant a play that ends happily, though it has tragic potentialities. But the modern attitude is totally different. It is a much more philosophical point of view than that of only form. It means a basic attitude of uncertainty about life itself. The writer asks: Is life ruled by 'chance' (arbitrarily) or by 'fate' (divine purpose)? He constructs his play accordingly. If he inclines towards the former then he shows the action and the characters as being ruled by arbitrary chances, coincidences, etc. and if he inclines towards the latter then he lays stress upon destiny or the gods' participation in determining these actions. In either case, it is a play full of doubt and uncertainty.

Mulryne, in addition, says that the dramatist just asks the question and never answers it, thus leaving the onus of interpretation on the reader. This too adds to the uncertainty. Thus in tragi-comedies there are two mutually opposing views of the world:

(1) That fate rules the world, usually a malevolent one. We are as Bosola says:

> merely the stars' tennis-balls, struck and banded
> Which way please them.[6]

(2) The second view is that it is arbitrary chance which rules the world. Here the element of coincidence gets preference. The fact that the Duchess and her family are banished from Ancona just at the point when she is away from all help is an instance of this.

This is the reason that the half-line Bosola utters gains such importance. The Duchess says she could curse the stars and Bosola says:

> Look you, the stars shine still[7]

This is a highly significant line for it can be interpreted in two ways, both fostering the tragicomic theme: (1) the stars go on giving light to mankind as Divine Purpose rules the world; (2) the stars are cruel and indifferent to man. They on shining, not caring for man's suffering. This possible double interpretation is the very essence of the theme of tragicomedies. This is also the essential spirit of our play.

Moreover, what makes up the modern spirit is the fact that often the writer does not take any of the two positions mentioned above. Instead of that he just puts the question: Is life ruled by divine purpose or by chance? He does not try to answer this question by adopting any of the views mentioned so far. If he did so, then at least it is a definite answer. Instead he is, as Mulryne says content just to question, leaving the reader to find his own answer. This is the stance adopted by modern writers like Beckett, Brecht, Ionesco and others. This highly ambiguous position however is not the one taken by our poet for whom an actively malevolent divine power rules the world.

(4) Melodrama of Defeat as the Theme

This is the concept expounded by James Smith. His idea of melodrama however, is very different from the conventional idea of it.

Melodramas became highly fashionable during the second half of the 19th century. At that time, plays were written that catered to the taste of the common public, not to the intelligentsia. These were plays with extravagant, exaggerated actions and language. The acting was in keeping with this sensationalism. The entire play was highly artificial and unrealistic. These plays came to be known as melodramas. They never got seriously regarded as literary works but were relegated to a definitely inferior status.

James Smith's idea of melodrama is totally different from this. Like Mulryne's idea of tragicomedy it is a philosophical interpretation of the spirit of melodrama. It is also different from the concept of tragedy. In tragedy, which is hero-centred, man is seen to be a being who is torn by a conflict. He is aware of his own imperfection. He knows what perfection is, but he also knows that he can never attain it. As Fulke Greville says in his famous chorus in his plays *Mustapha,* man is:

> Born under one law, to another bound.
> Vainly begotten, yet forbidden vanity,
> Created sick, commanded to be sound.
> What meaneth nature by these diverse laws
> Passion and reason, self-division's cause?[8]

So, the tragic man is divided by a conflict raging within himself and his problems spring from within himself and this is the very essence of the spirit of tragedy according to Smith.

The theme of melodrama on the other hand is totally different. Unlike the tragic man, the melodramatic man is a whole man, totally good, sure and also confident of himself. He knows fully well what is right and what is wrong. All the obstacles he has to face come from outside. He either overcomes them or is overcome by them. There are thus, three kinds of such plays:

(1) the melodrama of success

(2) the melodrama of defeat

(3) the result is stalemate, where neither happens.

According to Smith, the play under discussion is a melodrama of defeat. The theme is that of a totally good, whole and sound heroine's overcoming by malignant fate through no fault of her own. She knows what is right and what is wrong, there is no conflict in her. But she is overpowered by dangers that come from outside. The theme is thus of a melodrama of defeat.

(5) The Theme of Domesticity

As has already been elaborated before (Chap. 3), Elizabethan tragedies have been divided into four categories and the domestic tragedy is one of them. There are many plays of this kind (*Othello* being one) and the best of them are *Arden of Faversham* (1592) and *A Woman Killed With Kindness* (1607). These plays are all entirely domestic and familial in action and character, concerning a family and no more. They give a living picture of the life lived by ordinary people of those times, excluding the nobility and the aristocracy. They are the precursors of the modern kitchen-sink drama that are also realistic and domestic.

But this feature is not so important for the present play, for here the very highest level of aristocracy, the sovereign ruler of a state, is involved. But there are a few other features of such plays. Along with the death of the principal character, a problem of some kind is also involved. It is the supposed infidelity of Desdemona that is the problem in *Othello* which is also labelled as a domestic tragedy. The problem is not accompanied with violent or sensational incidents. Herein, this kind of tragedy is different from the revenge tragedy. The theme of domesticity is more highlighted by the plot construction of the play as there are two or more plots interacting with each other, all emphasizing its domestic nature. The Othello-Desdemona plot and the Cassio-Bianca plot in *Othello* are both domestic ones. The end is tragic and thus it differs from the modern kitchen-sink play.

This label has been put on our play also. But there are some reservations. Out of the features given above, only a few are to be found in it. It is not concerned with ordinary people but the sovereign ruler of a country. This is emphasized again and again:

> Why should only I
> Of all the other princes of the world
> Be cas'd up like a holy relic?[9]

The two brothers belong to the same level. In addition, the Cardinal belongs to the highest level in the church as a Cardinal is next in position to the Pope. It is out of the Cardinals that the Pope is chosen.

There is no problem here that has got to be solved. Any widow can remarry, and the Duchess's marriage is legally valid. As she points out:

> Why might not I marry?
> I have not gone about in this to create
> Any new world or custom.[10]

There is no valid answer to this except the maniacal jealousy of Ferdinand, so all he can do is to go on blaming her. Actually, her marriage is not a problem at all.

Both the plots, if the Cardinal-Julia intrigue can be called a plot, emphasize the domestic theme of the play. Here too, we find the flirtatious nature of Julia gain the upper hand in bringing about her downfall. She is attracted to Bosola and starts a flirtation with him:

> Julia: Yes, confess to me
> Which of my women 'twas you hir'd to put
> Love powder into my drink?
>
> Bosola: Love powder?
>
> J.: Yes, when I was at Malfi,
> Why should I fall in love with such a face else?
> I have already suffered for thee so much pain.[11]

This flirtatious bantering to which he replies in kind after having recovered from his first surprise is entirely domestic in nature. It does not involve very high-level characters for both of them can be called upper middle class characters, presents a problem and is entirely domestic in nature, involving a mere love-affair and that too a spurious one. There is no nobility about this intrigue. But it interacts with the main plot, emphasizing its domestic nature.

Our play differs in a significant manner from the domestic tragedies in that it is full of sensational incidents which is a feature of revenge plays, rather than of domestic ones. Herein, the theme of domesticity is distinct for no one can imagine the sensational death of Julia and the sufferings inflicted upon the Duchess to be of ordinary domestic nature. This is a most significant deviation from the traditional domestic tragedy. Otherwise the theme of domesticity is maintained throughout the play.

References

1. I : i : 315-24, p. 45.
2. II : v : 62-64, p. 69.
3. III : ii : 98-100, p. 76.
4. III : ii : 127-30, p. 77.
5. Bradbrook, M.C., *op. cit.*, p. 177.
6. V : iv : 59-60, p. 131.
7. IV : i : 97, p. 97.
8. Quoted by Theodore Spencer in *Shakespeare and the Nature of Man*, New York, 1945, p. 46.
9. III : iii : 128-30, p. 77.
10. III : ii : 98-100, p. 76.
11. V : ii : 151-56, p. 120.

6

The Major Characters

A successful play is one that has been proved to be stage-worthy. It is declared to be a classic when it has passed the far more difficult test of time. Our poet, Webster, is easily a classic in both these respects. His three main plays have given us some characters who are more than realistic convincing human beings as they often have symbolic dimension, and so become universal figures. There are many dramatists who depict their central figures with zest but keep their other minor figures, vague and shadowy. Marlowe is an example of this kind. Our dramatist however, depicts his characters, in the three major plays, with individualization, giving them a personality that is their own.

In these three tragedies he has given us some memorable characters. His tragic protagonists, like Vittoria, the Duchess and some others have decidedly, become immortal. Other dramatists (like Shakespeare) have given us more of them. But his protagonists are indelible figures, though few.

The most remarkable feature in his dramatic career is that he did not reach a point of stasis, especially in these plays. As he took up each play, his understanding of all human beings grew and so his delineations become more and more complex, and also detailed. His range and variety grew with each play. The very inmost depths of the human mind were plumbed, and all the complexities explored. His delineation of the mind that is abnormal and maniacal is specially remarkable in the present context.

Before studying the individual characters, it will be fitting to make some general observations. The most important of them is the view of Una Ellis-Fermor according to which his characters can be taken to fall into a series of particular characters.

> When we think of Webster's characters, we find that, even in the limited group of the three main plays, there is a marked tendency for them to fall into series.[1]

She finds several such groups among the male as well as the female characters:

(1) The group of "politicians," half stoic, half Machiavellian.

(2) Strong masculine quality in female characters.

(3) More passive feminine quality in female ones.

(4) Chorus characters.

Taking the groups one by one the first group is the most important. It begins with Flamineo in *The White Devil*, an imperfect bungler. In *The Duchess* we have the complex and inconsistent malcontent in Bosola. This study is taken a step forward in the pure intellectual—the Cardinal who is the very personification of Machiavellian doctrine.

Rometio in *The Devil's Law-Case* is the instinctive and spontaneous plotter to whom evil is a natural spontaneous quality.

The second type of the strong-minded female is seen first in Vittoria and she reappears in a more resolute manner in Julia of *The Duchess*. The passive female character is seen first in Isabella in *The White Devil* and, again, far more strongly in the Duchess of the play under discussion.

Even the chorus characters show development in the different plays. Delio and Pescara are shown more clearly in the upright judge Crispiano in *The Devil's Law-Case*. They represent the honesty and rectitude of the straight, the wholesome characters.

Turning to the study of individual characters, the list as given in Dramatis Personae of the text will be followed. In it the characters are given for their appearance on the stage, and the same order will be followed here. In the list of the important female characters the name of the Duchess, of course, comes first and thus we will start our studies with her character.

The Duchess

Webster had followed the story as given by Painter's *Palace of Pleasure*, but he had not followed him very strictly in drawing the characters. Here, specially in the study of the Duchess he had been inspired by Sir Philip Sidney's *Arcadia*. It has been pointed out by Allen that four characters of that book had served as models for the Duchess, specially Queen Erona.

Queen Erona, like the Duchess, had married beneath her and was imprisoned like her. Sidney says that she was:

> Sad indeed, yet one rather used than new fallen to sadness (as one who had the joys of her heart already broken seemed rather to welcome than to shun that end of misery.[2]

Again, a few pages later he says:

> ....glorying in the affliction and shunning all comfort, she seemed to have no delight but in making herself the picture of misery.[3]

This seems to be a perfect portrait of the Duchess, specially the Duchess of the prison scenes. But this will be discussed later.

To begin at the beginning, we have a picture of her even before she enters in the portrait drawn by Antonio. He is all admiration for her and sums up at the end of a passage fully 18 lines long:

> All her particular worth grow to this sum,—
> She stains the times past, lights the times to come[4]

So we know that he has whole-hearted admiration for her as a princess and as a woman. Then she enters and we have ample opportunity to see how justified his opinion is. As soon as she left with her brothers, they forbid her to marry and issue veiled threats to her. She does not show anger or impatience but agrees to their orders. This might make her seem to be too spiritless and meek, but this impression is seen to be false when in the next part of the same scene she woos and wins Antonio. In this charming scene she has a difficult task to perform: she has to make Antonio realize that she loves him. Gradually and very tactfully, she enchantingly does the wooing and marries him in the same scene. She says:

Go, go brag
You have left me heartless: mine is in your bosom.
I hope it will multiply love there[5]

A few lines later she says:

Awake, awake man
I do here put off all vain ceremony,
And only do appear to you a young widow
That claims you for her husband, and, like a widow
I use but half a blush in't[6]

A little later in the same scene they take marriage vows solemnly in the presence of the witness Cariola and according to the law of the time, are legally married.

This act of marriage needs several things. It needs courage to go against her brother's orders and tact in making Antonio realize she wants him. She proves she has both. She is not cowed by her brothers, nor is she uselessly coy. Webster gives an enchanting picture of her character in this scene.

After this we see her in many more scenes but the one in which another admirable trait is revealed is in Act III, sc. ii. This is the scene in which she comes to know that her brothers have come to know of her marriage. The quickness she shows here is admirable. She plans out that she will accuse Antonio of cheating her and banish him and tells him to take their first child and her jewels and seek refuge in Ancona where later she will join him. This excellent plan is quickly carried out. She tells Antonio:

The place you must fly to is Ancona;
Hire a house there; I'll send after you
My treasure and my jewellery.[7]

This quickness is truly admirable. Everything is planned out and done quickly.

But after this fortune fails her. In the scene at the shrine of Loretto she with her family is banished from Ancona. When she is away from all help and is at the mercy of her maniacal brothers. Then we have the prison scenes one after the other.

She is killed by strangling. Her attitude in these two scenes has been extensively commented upon in the scene-wise analysis of the play. Her character undergoes a radical charge, she becomes an infinitely noble character—so noble that it brings about a thorough change in the Machiavellian Bosola who becomes a normal human being, capable of pity, sympathy and admiration for nobility. He uses the word "noble" twice in four lines with reference to her. At first, she is rebelling against the malignant stars ("I could curse the starts") and then she becomes resigned to her fate. Here comes the famous passage:

> I am acquainted with sad misery
> As the tann'd galley-slave is with his oar.
> Necessity makes me suffer constantly
> And custom makes it easy[8]

Next she comes to the highest point in Christianity—she accepts her fate:

> Pull and pull strongly for your able strength
> Must pull down heaven upon me—
> Yet stay, heaven-gates are not so highly arch'd
> As princes' palaces, they that enter there
> Must go upon their knees (*kneels*)[9]

These highly spiritual lines have no equals in poetry before or since. Herein Webster has been inspired, as Allen has pointed out, by Queen Erona in Sir Philip Sidney's *Arcadia* from which the relevant lines have already been quoted above.

There are, all the same, several objections about the remarriage of widows which have been applied to the Duchess. M.C. Bradbrook cites several contemporary structures against such marriages and sums up:

> The point is that there are three reasons against the Duchess's marriage: She is a widow; she is of royal blood and has a duty to her rank; she acted simply on her likings, without advice, without the rites of the church and without publishing her marriage. Her brothers advance all three reasons but the second seems by far the most potent.[10]

Webster too pays attention to the second reason as is evinced by the Duchess' remark "He is basely descended" and the defence of it given by Bosola:

> Will you make yourself a mercenary herald
> Rather to examine men's pedigrees than virtues?
> You shall want him:
> For knowing an honest statesman to a prince
> Is like a cedar planted by a spring.[11]

The Duchess, in marrying beneath herself in an irresponsible manner, would come under the severest censure of the Church which, in the case of widow-marriage, required the widow to do penance.

According to Bradbrook, the Duchess develops from an irresponsible young girl into a noble figure when she realizes her mistake which after all is just class-consciousness and mere snobbery:

> It is through the awakening of responsibility that the Duchess develops into a tragic figure.[12]

Bradbrook's argument, though it might be supported by contemporary writings (and she cites many) that her tragic dignity depends on her recognition of a mistake she had made in marrying Antonio, however, is not supported by the play itself. She attains tragic dignity not through snobbery, but by a much higher factor, that of humiliation and acceptance of her fate as has been repeatedly pointed out.

Ferdinand

In the list of *dramatis personae* which is made according to the appearance of the character on the stage, the first name is that of Ferdinand. He is a truly repulsive person from any and all points of view. Even before he enters we have a character-sketch of both of them by Bosola:

> He and his brother are like plum-trees that grow crooked over standing pools; they are rich and over'aden with fruit, but none but crows, pies and caterpillars feed on them.[13]

That is to say, he is rotten through and through and this is a true estimate of both. When he enters with the others he is mixing with and talking to all in a jovial manner. Surrounded by flatterers, he encourages their sycophancy. Antonio, with true insight, gives a sketch:

...a most perverted and turbulent nature:
What appears in him mirth is merely outside;
If he laughed heartily, it is to laugh
All honesty out of fashion.[14]

This evaluation goes on for sometime and every word of this devastating criticism is true.

His next action confirms Antonio's opinion of him. He gets for Bosola the provisorship of her horses and as soon as he has got, it bribes him to spy on the Duchess. Bosola at first draws the line at spying but he persuades him by telling him of the job he has got for him. This is the first instance we have of his duplicity and the extremely dishonourable aspect of his nature.

Then comes the famous passage in which the two brothers, speaking by twin and interrupting each other, warn the Duchess against remarriage. This passage has been quoted before and it makes clear the causeless vindictiveness of his nature.

Nothing can govern his unequalled rage at learning the news that the Duchess has given birth to children. He at once conveys the news to the Cardinal.

I have this night digg'd up a mandrake
....
—a sister damn'd, she's loose i' the hilts;
Grown a notorious strumpet.[15]

As to why he should instantly call her a strumpet there is no valid reason except the vileness of his own nature. He grows so intemperate and vulgar that the cardinal becomes scornful of him. He says, in violent passion:

...here is the cursed day
To prompt my memory and here 't shall stick
Till of her bleeding heart I make a sponge
To wipe it out.[16]

It is in this scene that he first talks of revenge (though in a different way):

I would kill her now
In you or in myself; for I do think

It is some sin in us heaven doth revenge
By her.[17]

He of course means "revenge" in a different way, but it is significant that he uses the word at all as it reflects on some sin in the two of them. It actually is exactly that: his sinful, incestuous but completely unrecognized love for his own twin sister.

After this, his torturing of the Duchess starts. He derives extraordinary sadistic pleasure in inflicting all manner of torture on her. His own retribution starts after he sees her dead face:

Cover her face: mine eyes dazzle: she died young.[18]

Then he is as intemperate in his grief as he had been in his sadism. He accuses Bosola of having killed her. When Bosola tells him that he had only carried out his own orders he lashes out at him:

Mine! was I her judge?
Did any ceremonial form of law
Doom her to not being?[19]

After this we see him become subject to lycanthropy. It is his own nature that has how manifested itself as he had been like a wolf by nature. It is only at the last moment, just before dying, that he gets his sanity back:

My sister, O my sister! there's the cause on 't.[20]

Webster thought and the contemporary reader also did, that he had been punished as he deserved. But actually it is not so. By becoming mad he has actually escaped punishment as he is no longer conscious of his heinous crime. He should have been kept alive, in full consciousness of his crime, suffering searing agony every moment of his life. That would have been his punishment. Webster gives him the easy way out which he does not deserve.

The Cardinal

The name coming after that of Ferdinand in Dramatist Personae, the second such name, is that of the Cardinal. He, the brother of Ferdinand, is a far more formidable person than Ferdinand in that he is always controlled and never loses his temper as Ferdinand does. He is ruled by his intellect just as Ferdinand is ruled by his passions. He never loses control over himself. When Ferdinand is in one of his ungovernable rages, he repeatedly asks him to control himself. Antonio gives us a shrewd sum-up of his character.

> He is a melancholy churchman; the spring in his face is nothing but the engendering of toads.... He should have been Pope; but instead of coming to it by the primitive decency of the church, he did bestow bribes so largely....[21]

In other words, he is one who is also rotten through and through.

After this we meet him with Julia in Act II, sc. iv. Here he makes it clear to her that he no longer loves her and in the next scene (Act II, sc. v). Ferdinand discloses the fact of the birth of children to the Duchess. The Cardinal tells him again and again to control himself:

> I can be angry
> Without this rapture: there is not in nature
> A thing that makes man so deformed, so beastly,
> As doth intemperate anger.[22]

Later in the dumb show he gets the Duchess banished from Ancona but he takes no part in her imprisonment, torture and murder. That is left to his maniacal brother. Then he kills Julia by the ingenious contrivance of making her kiss the poisoned Bible. Here he commits two crimes, sacrilege and murder. His punishment starts in Act V, sc. v:

> How tedious is a guilty conscience!
> When I look into the fish-pond in my garden
> Methinks I see a thing armed with a rake
> That seems to strike at me.[23]

It is the devil that strikes at a man with a rake. So the world is now a living hell for him.

After this there is very little he does. He sees his own brother become insane and still goes on trying to save the situation by devising various means and at last, in the confusion and darkness is killed by Bosola. He dies with repentance gnawing at him:

> And now, I pray, let me
> Be laid by and never thought of.[24]

Thus, ends the life that has thriven on crime and blasphemy and is rotten through and through, like that of his brother. The same observation can be made about him as had been made about his brother. Death is not a fitting punishment for him. He should have lived on with full consciousness of his guilt. That would have been a fitting punishment.

Antonio

The name that comes after that of the Cardinal is that of Antonio. The full name is Antonio Bologna and he is the steward of the Duchess's household.

He is the first important character to enter the stage. Delio is with him but Delio is more of a chorus character than one who takes part in the action. It appears from their talk that Antonio has for some time past, been in the French court, to study their manner of administration. Antonio is a very shrewd person who can sum other people's character faultlessly. Some of the most important passages in the play belong to him and nearly all passages dealing with shrewdest character-analyses. In the very first long speech of the play we have, besides an account of the admirableness of the French court, a description of what a court should be like:

> a prince's court
> Is like a common fountain whence should flow
> Pure silver drops in general, but if 't chance
> Some curs'd example poison 't near the head
> Death and disease through the whole land spread.[25]

This very evaluation itself highlights his own honesty and nobility. Besides the Duchess, he is the only person who is wholly good. Only a man who is inherently honest and good can speak in this manner of a prince's court. As the play goes on, we get the picture of the main characters in it, each of them realistic, level-headed and proper sum-up of the person analysed. We have this picture of Bosola:

> Here comes Bosola
> The only court-gall, yet I observe his railing
> Is not for simple love of piety:
> Indeed he rails at those things which he wants,
> Would be as lecherous, covetous or proud

> Bloody or envious as any man,
> If he had means to be so.[26]

This is a true picture of Bosola. Of course, he develops into a far more complex figure later.

Then we have his opinion of the Cardinal. It is in prose and a true estimate:

> He is a melancholy churchman; the spring in his face is nothing but the engendering of toad.[27]

The analysis goes on for some more lines, describing how the Cardinal surrounds himself with flatterers and is himself a thoroughly corrupt man. His picture of Ferdinand is no less acute:

> a most perverse and turbulent nature
> What appears in him mirth is merely outside
> If he laughs heartily, it is to laugh
> All honesty out of fashion.[28]

One might think, from these three pictures, that he himself is a disagreeable person, who cannot see good in any one. This would be a mistake, for his appreciation of the Duchess is whole-hearted. He praises her virtues as well as her beauty and concludes:

> All her particular worth grow to this sum,—
> She stains the times past, lights the time to come.[29]

It is not surprising therefore that the Duchess should have but very little difficulty in persuading him to marry her.

He is purely a good character and after this scene this impression persists to the end. He does not develop any more. The Duchess is also a purely good character, but her personality goes on developing till the very end. This is because a spiritual dimension is added to her character. The same cannot be said of Antonio. His is not a complex character and there is no spiritual dimension to him. The fact that the Duchess chooses him for her husband is itself indicative of his goodness.

Bosola

Bosola without doubt is the most complex character in the play and one of the most complex in Elizabethan drama. He is introduced by Antonio as a typical Machiavellian malcontent person, "the only court-gall" who is ready to do anything at the two brothers' bidding and at first that is truly the impression he gives. He had taken some guilt of the Cardinal upon himself and served a sentence of two years in the galleys and is now back again. The first flash of individuality apart from that of a malcontent is seen when he refuses to spy upon the Duchess:

> Take your devils
> Which men call angels: these curs'd gifts would make
> You a corrupt, me an impudent traitor;
> And should I take these, they would take me to hell.[30]

This strain of honesty will make his salvation later on, but at present Ferdinand threatens and cajoles him into taking on the job.

Act II, sc. i, in which we see him next merely reveals his nature as a bitter malcontent. It is significant because of his revelation of his vision of man:

> Man stands amaz'd to see his deformity
> In any other creature but himself.
> ....
> And though we continually bear about us
> A rotting and dead body, we delight
> To hide it in rich tissue.[31]

After this when the Duchess comes, he tells us that he suspects her to be pregnant and brings on her birth-pains by giving her apricots to eat.

In the next scene, he is sure of the Duchess's pregnancy and in the scene after that (Act II, sc. iii) he gets hold of the all-important paper, the new-born baby's horoscope. He at once decides to send the news to the two brothers and does so.

We see him next a few scenes later, in Act IV, sc. iii. By this time the Duchess has had three children, and he tells Ferdinand this, though the father's name is not known. He comes to know it in Act III, sc. ii by praising Antonio to the Duchess till she tells him that it is he who is her husband.

It is from Act III, sc. v that he changes, taking on a complex dimension. Here, he becomes the prison-guard of the Duchess and is already so ashamed to face her that he wears a mask. He tries again and again to change the mind of the Duchess towards Antonio, and points out that he is not of noble descent.

Next come the two famous prison-scenes. Here his transformation is complete. He has been changed from a malcontent into a decent human being with the qualities of pity, sympathy and admiration for nobility. As Ferdinand asks him how the Duchess is bearing herself he says: "Nobly" and uses the word "noble" twice in 4 lines in describing her. When she enters the stage, he greets her with great respect and tries to comfort her: "All comfort to your grace." It is here that he utters the famous half-line:

> Look you, the stars shine still.[32]

This can be interpreted in two ways as has already been pointed out.

After this, as Ferdinand has denied her the comfort of a priest Bosola takes on the sacred task of a priest of preparing a condemned person for death. A priest chants in Latin but as he is not one, he cannot do so. So he chants some couples. The concluding lines are given here:

> Strew your hair with powder sweet
> Don clean Linen, bathe your feet
> And (the foul fiend more to check)
> A crucifix let bless your neck.
> 'Tis now full tide 'tween night and day;
> End your groan and come away.[33]

After the Duchess is killed, he cannot keep quiet any longer but speaks his mind to Ferdinand:

> Other sins only speak; murder shrieks out:
> The element of water moistens the earth
> But blood flies upward and bedews the heaven.[34]

Later when Ferdinand accuses him of murder and also talks wildly, he has no hesitation in laying the blame at his door. Then when he goes out, he does his best to revive the Duchess and when she is really dead, he, a changed man vows to avenge her murder.

In Act V, sc. ii he is in Rome and Julia flirts with him:

J.: Which of my women 'twas you hir'd to put
Love-powder into my drink

B.: Love-powder?[35]

At first he is taken aback ("Love-powder?") but he quickly understands Julia's game and flirts with her with the intention of using her to find out the cause of the Cardinal's melancholy. Then he goes out and a few lines later in the same scene the Cardinal kills Julia by making her kiss the poisoned Bible. Then when in the same scene Bosola enters the Cardinal tells him to hide the body and, promising him great honour, makes him promise to kill Antonio. As soon as he goes out Bosola, in a soliloquy, reveals his thoughts:

Well, good Antonio
I'll seek thee out, and all my care shall be
To put thee into safety from the reach
Of these most cruel brothers
....
I'll join with thee in a most just revenge
....
O Penitence, let me truly taste thy cup,
That throws men down only to raise them up.[36]

The next scene is the one in which in darkness he mistakes Antonio for Ferdinand and kills him, the one man he wants to save above all. It is here that he perceives the presence of a malevolent fate and speaks the famous lines:

We are merely the stars' tennis balls, struck and banded
Which way please them.[37]

These famous lines give us Webster's tragic vision—that mankind is pursued by an actively malevolent fate—the gloomiest view of man's fate to be found in tragedy, specially Jacobean tragedy.

Then in the darkness, he, the Cardinal and Ferdinand fight and give each other his death wound. With his last breath, he explains the whole thing to the chorus characters who have gathered around them and then gives voice again to Webster's own tragic vision:

O this gloomy world!
In what a shadow or deep pit of darkness
Doth womanish and fearful mankind live!
Let worthy minds never stagger to distrust
To suffer death or shame for what is just:
Mine is another voyage.[38]

These lines have been much commented upon, as has already been mentioned. What the last half-line means is ambiguous. Perhaps, it means that Bosola dies in uncertainty of his after-life, in the modern tragi-comic sense, not the Jacobean sense.

References

1. Ellis Fermor, U. *op. cit.*, p. 176.
2. Allen, *op. cit.*, p. 16.
3. *Ibid.*
4. I: i: 214-15, p. 41.
5. I: i: 441-43, p. 49.
6. I: i: 448-52, p. 50.
7. III: ii: 163-66, p. 79.
8. IV: ii: 27-30, p. 100.
9. IV: ii: 224-28, p. 106.
10. M.C. Bradbrook, *op. cit.*, p. 201.
11. III: ii: 251-55, p. 82.
12. Bradbrook, *op. cit.*, p. 203.
13. I: i: 50-53, p. 36.
14. I: i: 175-78, p. 40.
15. II: v: 1-4, p. 67.
16. II: v: 13-16, p. 67.
17. II: v: 61-64, p. 69.
18. IV: ii: 258, p. 108.
19. IV: ii: 294-96, p. 109.
20. V: v: 79, p. 135.
21. I: i: 162-71, p. 40.
22. II: v: 53-56, p. 69.
23. V: v: 4-7, p. 132.
24. V: v: 97-98, p. 136.

25. I: i: 11-15, p. 15.
26. I: i: 22-28, p. 36.
27. I: i: 163-65, p. 40.
28. I: i: 173-76, p. 40.
29. I: i: 214-15, p. 41.
30. I: i: 264-67, p. 43.
31. II: i: 56-64, p. 53.
32. IV: i: 98, p. 97.
33. IV: ii: 186-89, p. 105.
34. IV: ii: 255-57, p. 108.
35. IV: ii: 152-53, p. 120.
36. V: ii: 339-49.
37. V: iv: 59-60, p. 131.
38. V: v: 108-13, p. 136.

7
The Minor Characters

There are but a few dramatists who, like Shakespeare, take pains over their minor characters. Webster, however, in the three main plays, does take the trouble to give convincing portraits of his minor characters as well as the major ones. In his city comedies this is not the case—they are written in a more or less slipshod manner. But in these three major plays he does not neglect the minor ones altogether. In the *Duchess*, there are quite a few minor characters who are depicted with care. In looking at them, the same order will be followed as in the former chapter, that is, according to the order in which they are given in the list of the *Dramatis Personae*. In it they are mixed up with the major ones. They will be picked out one by one.

Delio

The first minor character to be found in the list is Delio and it is most appropriate since he appears in the very first scene and in the last scene of the play, the speech which see the restoration of moral order in the play after all the horrifying incidents in it, is spoken by him. Besides this, he serves several functions in the play.

He is introduced as Antonio's friend and he has the honour of opening the play just as he is the one to speak the last speech. There is a tendency among critics to group him with the chorus characters but that will be a mistake—he is a character in his own right, however minor he might be. Throughout the play as has been pointed out, he serves many purposes. Here for example, he informs the audience that Antonio has just come back from the French court:

> You are welcome to your country, dear Antonio.
> You have been long in France.[1]

It is he who, later, informs the audience that Bosola had taken the blame for a murder perpetrated by the Cardinal and had served two years in the galleys. Then later, it is he who, by dint of questioning, draws from Antonio the several character-sketches of the main persons.

After this we see him in Act II, sc. i in which he comes to know that Antonio and the Duchess have been married for a long time. This is just before the birth of the first child. It is after the Duchess is taken ill and goes out that he is left alone with Antonio and they talk freely. Delio proves to be a tower of strength to him. He reminds Antonio of several tasks to do at this time which the Duchess had already planned for, like bringing a trusty midwife. When Antonio assures him that these have been done, Delio then gives him very good advice: Let it be given out that Bosola had poisoned her and therefore everyone is confined to his room for the night. This will ensure the Duchess the privacy she needs. This is good advice and Antonio needs the steadying influence for he is in a very worried state.

In Act II, sc. iii, talking to Antonio, it is he who gives us the information that the Duchess is quite well. Again, he reassures Antonio, one who is suffering from many superstitions.

We see him next in Act II, sc. iv, directly after the Cardinal has made it clear to Julia that he is not in love with her. After he leaves Delio enters and as he had formerly been a suitor of hers, she starts at once to flirt with him. Delio shows himself susceptible to her suggestions. While he is with her, he hears that her husband has brought a letter for Ferdinand which has disturbed him and this makes him suspect Antonio is betrayed.

In Act III, sc. i, only he and Antonio are present on the stage at first. He had not been at Malfi for quite some time and Antonio is very relieved to see him. Again he serves the important function of eliciting the information from him that Ferdinand is behaving very strangely and dangerously. But he is confident that the two brothers do not know anything about his marriage with the Duchess. Indeed this, as has already been said, is one of his main functions in the play. Antonio tells him many items of information as well as his own sentiments and thus these become known to the audience. But it has to be remembered that he is not just a passive recipient of information, but in many cases, he advises and reassures Antonio too.

In Act III, sc. iii he gives a good impression of Malatesti's character in his talk with Silvio and later a description of Bosola as a scholar who is interested in esoteric things in philosophy and literature:

> ...a fantastical scholar, like such
> who study to know how many knots were
> there in Hercules's club, of what colour
> Achilles's beard was...and he did this
> to gain the name of a speculative man.[2]

This is a new aspect of Bosola of which the audience did not know anything so far. Nor will it be talked about later on. Delio is the only one who tells us about this aspect of Bosola.

After this there is a long interval before we see him again. Meanwhile the Duchess's torture and murder has taken place. We see him talking with Antonio in Act V, sc. i. In this scene, he tries to safeguard Antonio's interests, i.e. his property as much as he can. For example, meeting Pescara he asks him to bestow on himself Antonio's landed property.

> There is the citadel of Saint Bennet
> With some demesne, of late in the possession
> Of Antonio Bologna,—please you bestow them on me.[3]

But it is given to Julia, he does not get it. This happens in front of Antonio and when Julia goes out he once more assures him of his help:

> I will second you in all danger; and however
> My life keeps rank with yours.[4]

After this we see him next in the famous echo scene (Act V, sc. iii). He explains the properties of the fortification to Antonio (and to the reader also):

> ...and withal
> So plain in the distinction of our words

That many have supposed it is a spirit
That answers.[5]

At the end of the scene when Antonio is very anxious and downtrodden he proposes that he will bring his eldest son to the Cardinal as this might soften his heart. But before he comes back with the child everybody concerned is dead. So the sacred task of seeing the establishment of justice, of order being restored falls upon him. This extremely serious speech is delivered by him:

Let us make noble use
Of this great ruin; and join all our force
To establish this young hopeful gentleman
In his mother's rights.
....
Integrity of life is fame's best friend.
Which nobly, beyond death, shall crown the end.[6]

These are the last lines of the play. It should be remembered that Delio was the one to open the play in the first scene and to him falls the signal honour of delivering the last crucial speech.

Castruccio, Pescara, Malatesti, Roderigo, Grisolan

These are all chorus characters. They take very little part in the action, except to fill the stage and to represent popular opinion. Some of them have a line or two to speak in different scenes. Their main function is to express the opinion of the ordinary people.

The Two Pilgrims

These two pilgrims enter the stage only in Act III, sc. iv in which the Cardinal is invested as a warrior and the Duchess is banished from Ancona. All this happens in dumb show and the two pilgrims, representing ordinary people, are the only ones who speak in the beginning and at the end of the scene. It ends with a Senecan couplet by the first pilgrim:

Fortune makes this conclusion general
All things do help the unhappy man to fall.[7]

The Doctor

The Doctor is a very minor character and appears in one scene only (Act V, sc. iii). But in that one scene he takes a very important part, as it is he who diagnoses the disease Ferdinand is suffering from and explains its nature to Pescara (and to the audience):

> A very pestilential disease, my lord
> They call lycanthropia
> ....
> In those that are possessed with it there overflows
> Such melancholy humour they imagine
> Themselves to be transformed into wolves.[8]

It is explained much more in detail, over more than 20 lines. Later when Ferdinand comes in and tries to throttle his own shadow, he starts his treatment. It is a psychological treatment at first. He tries first to humour him like a child and then tries to frighten him and finally talks of starting other kinds of treatment. He gives the impression of being a dutiful conscientious man who is as learned as it was possible for a doctor to be in those days. He speaks with authority and it is noticeable that though he is socially inferior the lords all accept his authority.

Cariola

Cariola is the companion, the trusted maid of honour of the Duchess. She loves the Duchess and is trusted and loved in return. She is always with the Duchess and does not have a scene to herself. She speaks very little in the first scene—only to tell Antonio that the Duchess wants to see him in half an hour's time. Then when the two brothers leave after warning the Duchess against remarriage, she confides in Cariola, requiring her secrecy she says:

> I'll conceal this secret from the world
> As warily as those that trade in poison
> Keep poison from their children.[9]

She only comes out at the end of the scene to act as witness to their marriage. In those days, marriage vows taken in all solemnity in the presence of a witness made it a legally valid marriage. Cariola is the one who makes the marriage such a one. The last words of the scene are spoken by her: how she honours as well as pities the Duchess.

She is the one who in Act II, sc. ii tells Antonio that he is the father of a son:

> Sir, you are the happy father of a son
> Your wife commends him to you.[10]

We meet her next in Act III, sc. ii which in the beginning is an entirely domestic scene between husband, wife and maid. There is much light-hearted talk in the scene and Cariola speaks as the equal of Antonio and the Duchess. Then, after Ferdinand has come and gone Antonio and she come in. Antonio suspects her of having betrayed them to Ferdinand. She says:

> Pray Sir, do so; and when
> That you have cleft my heart you shall read there
> Mine innocence.[11]

We can take each word of this to be true and he too realizes this.

Her next significant appearance is in Act IV, sc. ii which is the scene in which the murder of the Duchess and her own take place. There is the anti-masque of madmen in the scene at the beginning and when the Duchess, hearing the noise they are making wants to know its cause Cariola tells her that Ferdinand has got hold of these madmen to torture her:

> this tyranny
> I think, was never practis'd till this hour[12]

She tries to console the Duchess and cheer her up:

> You shall live
> To shake this durance off.[13]

A little later the Duchess asks her what she is looking like, and she tells her that she looks like her portrait, and then with true insight she says:

> Or rather like some reverend monument
> Whose ruins are even pitied.[14]

Then later she realizes that the Duchess is going to be killed and declares "I will die with her." When the executioners kill the children, she realizes that her own time has come and says, with a nobility like the Duchess's own:

> My turn is next
> Is it not so order'd?[15]

At the last moment, she tries to escape death by telling Bosola that she is engaged, then she tells him that she has not been to confession and then that she is pregnant. Nothing avails and she is strangled.

She is, thus, loyal to the Duchess till the very end and does really die for her. She stays with her till the very end and, till the very end, tries to console her. Hers is, from this point of view, a very important role. At the last moment, when everyone else has gone, the Duchess has only her to stay with her and die for her—a truly unique role.

Julia

Julia's name comes next to Cariola's. She is the wife of Castruccio and more important than that, the mistress of the Cardinal. Her first significant appearance is in Act II, sc. iv. In this scene, the Cardinal makes it clear to her that he no longer wants her as he used to. She herself speaks very little in this scene, mostly half lines. There is no need for her to speak, she understands the Cardinal only too well. She does not cry out or weep piteously or reproach him. Instead, she withdraws in a calm and dignified manner.

Later in the same scene when Delio enters she talks to him very graciously as he had in the past been one of her suitors. He offers her money to be his mistress which she rejects scornfully. She says with reference to the sound of gold:

> A lute-string far exceeds it:
> It hath no smell, like cassia or civet.[16]

She returns a non-committal answer to Delio's proposal and the scene ends. We meet her next after the murder of the Duchess when Ferdinand is already mad and Bosola has come to Rome in Act V, sc. ii. She sees Bosola and is attracted to him and starts flirting with him:

> Which of my women 'twas you hir'd to put
> Love-powder in my drink.[17]

Bosola shows himself to be well up in this game and there is a lot of badinage between the two. He asks her why the Cardinal is so melancholy and she tries to do so after he has left. As a result of her cajolery the Cardinal tells her about the murder of the Duchess, and she is horrified and confesses that she will not be able to keep the knowledge a secret. It is then that he kills her by making her kiss the poisoned Bible. When she dies, it is in a dignified manner:

> I forgive you
> This equal piece of justice you have done
> ....
> 'Tis weakness
> Too much to think what should have been done. I go
> I know not whither.[18]

Thus, ends a frivolous and useless life. But it has to be said that she never loses her dignity—not when she realizes the Cardinal's indifference to her, and nor when she dies.

Old Lady

She is a very minor character and we see her only in two scenes. The first time she is there only as a springboard for Bosola to give Castruccio his views on women. It is in Act II, sc. i that she comes first and Bosola's behavior to her is most discourteous. She hardly speaks in this scene and after Bosola has aired his views leaves the stage.

She is present again in Act II, sc. ii and this time she is present for some definite purpose. The Duchess's birth-pains have started and she is one of the ladies attending her. She speaks only a few sentences—four to be exact and Bosola does not know that she is attending the Duchess. But she is in haste and does not stop to talk to him. These are the only two times that she comes. We do not come to know everything about her.

These are the only minor characters worth mentioning. Besides them there are the madmen in the antimasque who are not worth discussion.

This account shows that Webster individualized his minor characters also, giving them due importance. He does not leave them as shadowy figures, dwarfed by the towering personality of the hero, nor does he give each of them the importance that Shakespeare gives. He gives each character as much as it deserves, neither more, nor less. His is the middle way, between Marlowe on one hand and Shakespeare on the other.

References

1. I: i: 1-2, p. 35.
2. III: iii: 40-46, pp. 85-86.
3. V: i: 19-21, p. 112.
4. V: i: 74-75, p. 114.
5. V: iii: 6-9, p. 127.
6. V: iv: 118-29, p. 137.
7. III: iv: 42-43, p. 88.
8. V: iii: 6-10, p. 115.
9. I: i: 346-49, p. 46.
10. II: ii: 77-78, p. 60.
11. III: ii: 104-06, p. 78.
12. IV: ii: 3-4, p. 99.
13. IV: ii: 11-12, p. 100.
14. IV: ii: 33-34, p. 100.
15. IV: ii: 234-35, p. 107.
16. II: iv: 62-63, p. 66.
17. V: ii: 151-53, p. 120.
18. V: ii: 281-89, p. 127.

8

Plot or Dramatic Strategies

Aristotle has named the plot as the first of the six essentials of tragedy. It is so very important that he has called it "the soul of tragedy". He had laid down many rules for the plot and the Elizabethan dramatists knew all of them quite well. We shall glance at a few of the important ones of them.

The Classical Rules

We have, first of all, to keep Aristotle's famous definition of tragedy in mind:

> Tragedy, then, is the imitation of an action that is serious, complete, and of a given magnitude; in language embellished with each kind of artistic ornament, the several kinds being found in separate parts of the play, in the form of action, not of narration; through pity and fear affecting the proper purgation of these emotions.[1]

Many later commentators have expounded the various complexities of this definition, into which we need not to go. This is to be treated as a point of reference for the rules to be explained now. All the features of tragedy that will be explained refer to it.

First of all, there are the well-known and most important rules about the plot, the three unities: (a) the Unity of Action, (b) the Unity of Time, and (c) the Unity of Place. The Elizabethans did not take them very seriously, nor did Webster.

The Unity of Action: This is the most important of the Unities. It refers directly to the definition he gave. He had said in the definition that the action of a tragedy is "serious" and this implies that there should be no mingling of serious and comic actions in a tragedy. Such a rule is specially relevant at present, as pity and terror, which are the emotions evoked by serious action, are the specific ones for tragedy. Webster observes this rule, for there are hardly any comic plots in the present play.

The Unity of Time: It is desirable that the time covered by the play should tally with the actual performance-time. This is almost impossible. Aristotle gives "a single revolution of the sun", i.e. one full day, for a play. This too is difficult, but not impossible as all of Ben Jonson's plays take just one day.

Webster does not care much for this rule. The action of *The Duchess of Malfi* take several years, for three children are born to the Duchess and the youngest is a few years old when she is killed. So, the entire action of the play takes a minimum of five to six years, though it is not very clear how long the two brothers live after this. Definitely long enough for Julia to be killed and the two brothers to be ill in Ferdinand's case and more plotting in the case of the Cardinal.

The Unity of Place: This rule means that all the action of a play should take place in one location. This rule, however, was not given by Aristotle himself. It came to English dramatists via the works of the Italian Renaissance like Minturno, Scaliger, Castelvetro and others who had misinterpreted Aristotle. This rule was also difficult to follow and the only dramatist to do so is Ben Jonson. It is more or less observed in this play. The changes of scene are not very frequent. Most of them, specially the important ones, take place in Malfi, though there is the scene at Loretto and some scenes in Rome too. The scenes after the Duchess's death take place at Rome.

There are many more rules that have been given by Aristotle that have been expounded by later scholars. One such famous scholar was Donatus whose treatise was a textbook in Elizabethan times. According to him the first part of a play is the Prologue. Usually this is a speech coming before the actual play starts. The Prologue in Marlowe's *Dr Faustus* is a good example of a prologue in the classical manner. The dialogue between Antonio and Delio in the present play constitutes its prologue.

Certain other classical rules are there. *Peripeteia* or Reversal is a very important one. This means the fall of the hero from a high station in life to a low one. According to Aristotle, the ideal plot of a tragedy is one that involves the fall of a rather good man from prosperity to adversity. It is definitely present in *The Duchess* for in it the sovereign ruler of a country is imprisoned like any felon and killed by common hangmen.

Anagnorisis or Recognition is also an important part of the tragic plot. At its most superficial level, it means the mutual recognition of two persons who had been separated, as happens in *Twelfth Night*. The most refined kind of *anagnorisis* occurs when a character recognizes his own nature. *Anagnorisis* of a very painful and subtle kind occurs in our play when at the end just before dying Ferdinand realizes his own sinful love for his sister.

Another important part of the plot is *Pathos* or the scene of suffering. This includes physical pain, death, etc. This is definitely present in our play in the prison-scenes, but Webster gives this element a new dimension by making the sufferings of the Duchess entirely mental and not physical. This psychological dimension is entirely his own.

Certain Elizabethan Features

Classical rules dictate that a tragedy should have only one plot. A sub-plot goes against the rules though intrigues are allowed. Sub-plots are allowed in comedies, specially in the new comedies but not in tragedies. But the Elizabethan dramatists started more than one plot in a tragedy. What is worse, the sub-plot is usually a comic one and so it violates the unity of action. This however is not the case in this play as in it the intrigue concerning the Cardinal and Julia cannot be called as a comic one.

In Elizabethan plays the different plots and intrigues are not just arbitrarily thrown together. Instead there is often a definite relationship between them even if there are many intrigues or sub-plots. This relationship can be of many types and has been studied in detail. This is so common a feature that it is difficult to find a play that has only one plot. All the plays of Ben Jonson who is a strict classicist, are multiple-plotted. Webster also, following the common trend of his time, has given the Cardinal-

Julia intrigue that repeats, in an entirely sordid way, the love interest of the main plot.

Another well-known feature of these plays is the element of the supernatural which has already been discussed earlier. It is present in the echo scene in an extraordinary manner. Aristotle called it the element of "the marvellous" and recognized its importance:

> The marvellous should be represented in tragedy.... The marvelous is a source of pleasure.[2]

In Greek tragedies, the marvellous is really a pleasure-giving phenomenon, so Aristotle regards it as such. But the Elizabethans used it to inspire fear and terror (e.g. *Macbeth*). The echo-scene in the present play is also used to produce fear and anxiety. In this instance, Aristotle has another valuable sentence:

> Probable impossibilities are to be preferred to improbable possibilities.[3]

Many theoretical works on the subject were available at that time. Ghosts, fairies and other such entities formed part of the beliefs, along with many superstitions concerning them. Some of the notable treatises were Reginald Scot's *Discovery of Witchcraft* (1584). Burton's *Anatomy of Melancholy* and Lewes Lavater's *Of Ghoftes and Spirites Walking by the Nyght*. These and many others were available to Webster. There was no dearth of material for him and other dramatists.

The presence of the supernatural is a must in all revenge tragedies and our play is regarded as one such. All the same there is a world of difference between Kyd's use of it and that of our poet. In the latter, we have no ghost crying out for "Revenge". Everything is so subtle that it is hardly recognizable as the same thing that was present in the earlier plays. This is clearly to be seen in the echo scene (Act V, sc. iii). It is definitely the element of the marvellous but so presented as to be almost natural, a "probable impossibility" according to Aristotle. First of all, it is a ruined fortification and Delio explains its properties to Antonio. The entire place is such that it throws back very distinct echoes:

And withal
So plain in the distinction of our words
That many have supposed it is a spirit
That answers.[4]

This echo scene, thus, adds a new dimension to the use of the supernatural in Jacobean drama—the "probable impossible" is superseded by that which is only too possible.

Another important feature of this drama is the use of soliloquies. Sometimes, they are so important that they supplant the action as is the case with *Hamlet*. In the present play, however, they are not very important. As a matter of fact, there are hardly any soliloquies in it. The one important soliloquy is the one spoken by Bosola after he has tried to revive the Duchess in Act IV, sc. ii. It is of twenty lines and very important as it presents the completely changed personality of Bosola. He vows to avenge her murder. There are tears in his eyes as he speaks:

O Sacred innocence that sweetly sleeps
On turtles' features, whilst a guilty conscience
Is a black register....
This is manly sorrow...where were
These penitent fountains while she was living?
O they were frozen up! Here is a sight
As direful to my soul as is the sword
Unto a wretch hath slain his father.[5]

This is the only soliloquy of note in the play and it is masterly in its revelation of character.

The Sources of the Play

Like most of the dramatists of the time, Webster did not invent the story of the play himself. He took it from Painter's well-known collection *Palace of Pleasure*. It is a moral story, told as warning to women against indulging in sensual pleasure. Webster followed the story as given by Painter down to the death of the Duchess, diverging a little from the original story. There are, however, many additions and alterations. The most important of these is the brothers' warning against remarriage and almost the whole of the Acts IV and V. The Duchess's torture, the antimasque of the madmen, Ferdinand's lycanthropia, etc. are all added by him. The echo scene, the intrigue between Julia and the Cardinal, everything is his addition. After making a long list of these additions, of which only a few have been mentioned above, Allen says:

> Of these additions to the plot a few are contributed for spectacular effects, for stage shows and processions, of which Webster seems to have been fond.[6]

The Plot

As has already been mentioned, there are many deviations from the original story. The most important problem we face in the plot of the play is the delay in revenge. The brothers come to know about the birth of the first child almost immediately, but they take action after the third child is born. No satisfactory reason for the delay can be found. Allen is of the opinion that Webster had suddenly changed his plan about the plot. Against this highly practical but unsatisfactory explanation can be put Una Ellis-Fermor's eminently philosophical explanation. She thinks that the plot is not a mere succession of events, but something like an adventure of the soul of each character concerned:

> The true plot of his play is not the events which proceed upon the surface and are flung off, as it were, as a casual expression, but the progress of the minds of the central figures towards deeper and deeper self-knowledge.[7]

Looked at from this point of view, the entire play is a study of characters, not events and this critic's study of the play is more a study of its characters than anything else.

M.C. Bradbrook, after making an extensive study of the play inclines a little towards Ellis-Fermor's view in that she thinks that much depends upon "the unity of tone and temper" and that this adversely influences the structure of the play. She utters a word of caution:

> In this respect the study of Webster should prove a corrective to those who hastily assume that poetic structure is a matter of choice of words only.[8]

John Russell Brown is of the opinion that the plot is a matter of contrasts and balances. This is a rather far-fetched and fanciful interpretation, but Webster is a poet, or rather, *The Duchess of Malfi* is a play whose tremendous impact makes readers fanciful. Brown gives many contrasts, the chiefest of which are:

Death of Cariola—the death of the Duchess.
Madmen loosed—the Duchess chained
Antonio feels danger—the Duchess looks for virtue.

As against this, there is Nigel Alexander. For him the action of the play depends upon the efforts made by the characters to conceal, or discover, two secrets—first the Duchess's marriage and the second, her murder. The Duchess and Antonio try their utmost to keep the secret of their marriage from the brothers. Bosola, on behalf of the brothers, tries to discover the same secret. This is the main concern in the first half of the play. After the Duchess's murder the emphasis falls on that. Now the brothers try to keep the secret and Bosola tries to reveal it. As Ferdinand becomes mad the responsibility of the secret falls on the Cardinal. Julia nags at him till he can keep the secret no longer, telling it to her under a sacred oath. After that he kills her for fear, a just one, that she will reveal it. Thus, one crime leads to another. Bosola, trying to avenge the murder, decides to keep silent on the subject as it will help his pursuit of revenge and reveals the secret only at death's door, when it can harm or benefit, none.

The masque was a definite convention in those times. It was used for splendour and spectacle, with divinities, song and dance. Very often they were independent of the play, to heighten pleasure. Webster has done the opposite. It is part of his dramatic strategy to let realistic representations come in and contrast them with horror, as has been pointed out by Inga-Stina Ekeblad. He has taken the convention of a pleasant entertainment and turned it into a horror-show. It is actually an anti-masque and has been studied as such in detail. Realism and convention, according to her, has been fused together. Yet, as she shows, the structure of the conventional masque has been carefully followed. The dance of the madmen, she says "acts as an ideograph of the dis-unity, the incoherence of Webster's world".

References

1. S.H. Butcher, *op. cit.*, p. 23.
2. T.S. Dorsch ed. and transl., *Classical Literary Criticism*, Peng. Bks., 1975, p. 68.
3. *Ibid.*
4. V: iii: 6-9, p. 127.
5. IV: ii: 150-63, p. 111.
6. Allen, *op. cit.*, p. 5.
7. Ellis-Fermor, U., *op. cit.*, p. 276.
8. Bradbrook, M.C., *op. cit.*, p. 212.

9

Imagery in *The Duchess of Malfi*

Images are pictures made of words. In poetry they are used not only to beautify but also to make poetry more effective. They can be functional and decorative and much more. This aspect of poetry has been studied quite exhaustively by modern scholars. The relationship between images, their function, the creation of atmosphere and the theme, and the development of imagery in any work—all these have been studied and analysed.

Henri Fluchère's definition of imagery covers all its manifold aspects:

> Imagery may shortly be defined as a complete illustration drawn upon by the poet to clarify or embellish the object that he seeks to describe.[1]

This definition is quite comprehensive, yet it does not cover the scope of imagery effectively, for actually images have many functions in addition to these two. They can illustrate moods, foretell future events, reveal a character's mood, etc.

It is often impossible to distinguish between rhetorical figures, imagery and symbolism in poetry. This is because these three, besides being integrally related, often overlap. For example, an image can be studied as a figure of speech if expressed as such. It may also be a symbol. Fluchère has mentioned this as well:

> No strict rule allows us to say at what point we pass the plane of pure psychology, and even the metaphysical plane, in the use of imagery.[2]

The same image, again, can be easily categorized differently so that a sense image can also be a nature image or a domestic image or some other kind. It can happen to all images.

The most obvious categorization of images is according to the senses. That is to say, the five senses possessed by us. Thus:

Images related to the eye—visual images
Those related to the ears—auditory images
Those related to the nose—olfactory images
Those related to the tongue—gustatory images
Those related to the skin—tactile images

Such images may exist independently or may mix and mingle with others, and in that case, it will be known as synaesthesia.

However, strictly speaking, sense images can hardly ever exist independently, for they usually include some other aspect of life. Sense images are the most obvious ones and *The Duchess of Malfi* is rich in them. In the list of images to be given now, most of them will be taken from the first scene of the first Act for the sake of convenience. When, however, a particular point has to be illustrated, examples will be taken from elsewhere in the play, if necessary. The very first image is a visual one:

You have been long in France, and you return
A very formal Frenchman in your return habit.[3]

This is a visual image, for a habit (dress) is to be seen and at the same time a dress image also. But it is nothing extraordinary, for a visual image means that some object is being seen, so the image will be related to that object also. So, Antonio's description of the French court is a visual image:

-a prince's court
Is like a common fountain, whence should flow
Pure silver drops in general.[4]

This is a visual image because of fountain is to be seen. It is also an elemental image as it has to do with the element of water. It is also a simile and as it continues for a few more lines, it is a Homeric simile. It is a most effective image. Here, in addition to a visual image we have, a few lines later, the image of a poisoned land. Thus, an image hardly ever stands by itself.

Both of these are mainly visual images, but there are images pertaining to other senses as well. There is Bosola's famous description of the two brothers:

> ....they are rich and o'erladen with fruit but none but crows, pies and cater-pillars feed on them.[5]

Here the image is a gustatory one, concerned with eating. Then there are auditory images also. So Antonio speaks of Ferdinand:

> He speaks with others' tongue
> And hears men's suits
> With others' ears.[6]

Classical images are used very frequently. Bosola speaks thus of hope:

> What creature ever fed worse than
> hoping Tantalus? Nor ever died any man....[7]

This is a classical image as well as a gustatory one for Tantalus is always associated with thirst.

Different branches of knowledge are used to provide variety. When Bosola says:

> Take your devils
> which hell calls angels.[8]

He is here making use of religion, and of the names of gold coins that are called angels. In other words, two different branches of knowledge are used. When Ferdinand says:

> Hypocrisy is woven of a fine thread
> Subtler than Vulcan's engines.[9]

Here he is making use of a knowledge of classical myths and of spider's web, two utterly different branches of knowledge. We find many examples of this kind of composite images. An enchanting one is used by the Duchess:

> here upon your lips
> I sign your Quietus est. This you should have begg'd now.
> I have seen children oft eat sweetmeats thus
> As fearful to devour them too soon.[10]

This indeed is a very fine image. There is the phrase "Quietus est" which has double meaning: (1) it is associated with death and sacrifice as it is Christ's last words on the cross and (2) it is associated with law as it is used when accounts presented are found to be correct. This is concerned also with the gustatory image of children eating sweetmeats, and this is connected with the habit of little children, i.e. another different branch of knowledge. It is a very fine and complex image, religion, death, law, gustatory and paediatrics, all brought together harmoniously so that there is never any impression of complexity or farfetchedness.

H.T. Price has made a valuable survey of Webster's images. Right in the beginning of his essay he declares:

> I have chosen Webster to investigate because in the depth, the subtlety and the complexity of his images, he comes nearer than any other dramatist to the power of Shakespeare.[11]

First of all he points out that there is a stock of images available to all Elizabethan dramatists but Webster gave them a new interpretation, so that often they are ambiguous and have double significance. This critic calls it:

> his consistent use of a double construction, an outer and an inner. He gives us figure in action and figure in language.[12]

He also tells us that the function of imagery is the same as in all drama. First of all, "it is the most pregnant expression of truth", secondly it reveals character, thirdly it does the work of arguments, and lastly, it prefigures the events to come. Unfortunately he does not give any examples. There are so many examples but there is not any that fulfils all of these requirements. For example, when the Duchess says to Antonio:

> here upon your lips
> I sign your *Quietus est*.[13]

This is indeed a most complex image. It serves many of the functions pointed out by Price and in addition it is a religious image. But the most important function it serves is to foreshadow the future calamitous end of the love that is apparent here. Not all dramatists can foreshadow the future so effectively and so briefly. The echo-scene is also one that foreshadows the future. It is done most subtly.

Price divides Webster's imagery into two kinds: (a) figure in words and (b) figure in action. Analysing the first scene he says that Webster's ability to convey a multiplicity of meaning with the help of imagery is great. In the first eighty lines he has, through the images used by Antonio, given the picture of the corruption of the two brothers and has established the idea of (1) treachery, (2) poison and (3) corruption in separate individuals (the Cardinal, Ferdinand and Bosola). It is done in such a way that the lovers' trust in good fortune will prove to be entirely misplaced. There is irony to reinforce the imagery. This irony is brought home to us in the lines spoken by the Cariola at the end of the scene:

> Whether the spirit of greatness or of woman
> Reign most in her, I know not, but it shows
> A fearful madness. I owe her much of pity.[14]

The scope of imagery in the first scene is immense, and this critic calls it Webster's "Kaleidoscopic" vision which he shifts here and there and new implications, new glory bursts out. He traces this interplay of different kinds of images throughout the play. They are figure in action. Most of them, that is depend on the meaning of the words.

The best figure in action in the play is shown in the dumb show. Not a word is uttered during the show by the main characters. Yet the calamity in which the Duchess and her whole family is placed leaves no one in any doubt. During the show itself a solemn song is sung by churchmen which is ironic in the highest degree. The song prays for the safety and prosperity of a man who goes out to kill in the name of religion, a man who is evil through and through and who while going makes the torture and the murder of the Duchess possible. After going through the entire play this critic observes:

> Figure-in-action and figure-in-words reinforce one another. He repeats his theme tirelessly spinning innumerable variations.[15]

Here he also points out the irony inherent in the imagery, as Webster always shows up the shades of glory and magic as contrasting the inner corruption of the whole set-up.

Besides these many other theories concerning imagery have been expounded by critics. One such idea is that of "Iterative imagery" given by Caroline Spurgeon, that authoritative and pioneering spirit in the study of imagery. This concept of an image or several images being repeated throughout the play so as to make a pattern is entirely hers. This we can easily find in our play as the image of poison, corruption and death are repeated throughout the whole play. Images concerning corruption, death and poison as H.T. Price has already pointed out occur throughout. In the very first scene Antonio says:

> but if it chance
> Some curs'd example poison 't near the head
> Death and disease through the whole land spread.[16]

Accumulation of images gives depth and the desired complexity to poetry. In the famous ambition speech Antonio makes use of one image after another, thus heightening the effect:

> Ambition, madam, is a great man's madness
> That is not kept in chains and close-pent rooms
> But in fair lightsome lodgings and is girt
> With the wild noise of prattling visitants
> Which makes it lunatic beyond all care.[17]

Here we have an accumulation of images, all allied with the theme of madness. If anything can stand beside Macbeth's "To-morrow and to-morrow and to-morrow" passage, only this can.

W.H. Clemen has given three ideas concerning imagery: (1) image-consciousness, (2) image-complex, and (3) ambiguity. Not all of these are applicable to the present play, but the second, that of image-complex, is. Clemen has taken the idea from Caroline Spurgeon and explains it with reference to Shakespeare but it is equally applicable to Webster and indeed to any dramatist:

> In the case of image complex which lie close to Shakespeare's heart, such as gardening and plant-lore we often find that on each occasion only individual figures of speech are selected.[18]

In other words, many images concerning one idea are given. Thus, when the Duchess is proposing to Antonio she says about duplicity:

> We are forced to woo because none dare woo us
> And as a tyrant doubles with his words
> And fearfully equivocates, so we
> Are forced to express our violent passions
> In riddles and in dreams and leave the path
> Of simple virtue which is never made
> To seem the thing it is not.[19]

Here the main idea is duplicity because the Duchess is forced to take recourse to it, however unwillingly. So she refers to a tyrant, an equivocator, and speak of riddles, etc. which are all images to do with duplicity. There are indeed many such image-complexes.

Goethe had remarked upon animate and inanimate nature images. He had noticed a kind of co-operation between them. He wrote in particular about *A Midsummer Night's Dream* in this connection but the remark can be applied to all plays.

> Even the inanimate world takes part; all the subordinate things have their role, the elements, the phenomena of the heavens, the earth and the sea, thunder and lightning.[20]

There are many nature images in the play and they are always suited to man. There is the famous description by Bosola of the two brothers:

> He and his brother are like plum-trees that grow by standing pools; they are rich and o'erladen with fruit, but none but crows, pies and caterpillars feed on them.[21]

Here we have both animate and inanimate forms of nature. Standing pools are inanimate aspects of nature and plum-trees, pies and caterpillars are the animate ones. But in the context, they are not incongruous as they all reveal the nature of man, or, in Goethe's words there is "co-operation" between them. There are many such images in the play. What is remarkable is that they are not used to highlight or illustrate anything admirable and good. All the nature images used in the play, whether animate or not, co-operate with man to highlight his negative aspect only.

There is another characteristic of Shakespeare's images to which Clemen draws attention that can be applied to Webster. It is the use of metaphor along with imagery:

> he combines the abstract with metaphorical attributes without compunction. Thus a peculiar world is created in which the concrete is continually mingling with the abstract.[22]

There are many examples of this in our play. Thus Ferdinand says to the Duchess:

> Hypocrisy is woven of a small fine thread
> Subtler than Vulcan's engines.[23]

Here hypocrisy is an abstract quality but it is mixed up with Vulcan's engine which is a concrete thing. This is mixed up with classical allusion, which is a different matter, making the lines memorable.

Thus it can be seen that Webster does not lag behind the other dramatists in the matter of imagery. In fact, he is the only one who can stand beside Shakespeare in this.

It is a remarkable fact that the images cited so far have all had rather unpleasant associations. This does not, however, mean that the dramatist does not give pleasant or attractive images. From the first scene to the very last, there are as will be tried to show now, many nice, many attractive and pleasant images throughout the play. The very first image in the play is a pleasant one. But it is a long one and can easily be divided into two parts. As a matter of fact, the dramatist has done exactly this, for he has put a comma in between the two halves, thus leaving the reader in no doubt about his intention. It is in the second part that the image comes to have unpleasant associations, but the first part is an emphatically lovely one. This, however, is not usually noticed because the critics always, paradoxically, lay more emphasis on the second part:

> Considering duly that a prince's court
> Is like a common fountain, whence should flow
> Pure silver drops in general,[24]

It ought to be noticed here that the dramatist gives a comma at the end of this part of the quotation, and the second part with unpleasant associations, starts after the punctuation mark: "but if't chance" etc. So far as this one goes, however, it is definitely a pleasant image, an elemental one because it is the element of water that is concerned—water that preserves life and purifies us. It purifies us not in just a worldly sense (cleaning dirty things, like clothes, by washing them in water) but in a spiritual sense as well. When a priest takes holy water and sprinkles it over us, human beings, it cleanses off our spiritual uncleanliness. When the priest sprinkles in the rooms of a house, taking the names of the Father, the Son and the Holy Ghost while doing it, that house is purified of spiritual uncleanliness. Ghosts, Pohergeists, etc. will not be able to visit it. Thus water is the purest thing in the world. As used by the dramatist here, it is the very symbol of purity, definitely an image which is not just pleasant, but the very symbol of elemental purity. It is a visual image, as water can be seen, a tactile image, as it can be touched, and an auditory image, as the water of a fountain usually flows with a tinkling sound.

We find our next pleasant image in the same scene. It is a long and a very important scene, infact, and in the course of this discussion it will be seen that there are many lovely images in it, almost as many as ugly, unattractive ones. Here Ferdinand is talking to lords attending upon him. He says about a bird, referring to Pliny the famous classical writer, that, like him:

> I think he was begotten by the wind, he runs as if he were ballasted with quicksilver.[25]

Here, we have two very attractive and effective images: (1) that the bird is begotten by the wind, (2) that it is supported by mercury. The first of the images is an animal image and an elemental one: bird and the wind, and the second is that of quicksilver or mercury. To imagine, with Pliny as is given in the text itself, that it was begotten by the wind, an element known for its clarity and speed and strength, is in itself beautiful and then to imagine it being supported by that most mysterious of all metals, quicksilver, is even more so because quicksilver is sacred to the classical god, Mercury, the god of speed and of healing, it is liquid, but a metal all the same—most mysterious. Pliny, the classical naturalist, wrote a book named *National History*, which was available to the dramatist as well as his contemporaries, in the original as well as in translation. It is not surprising that he should refer to it.

Then, about a page later Antonio refers to the Greek myth of the Trojan horse, described by Homer and others:

> Nobly, my lord: as out of the Grecian horse issued many famous princes, so out of brave horsemanship arise the first sparks of growing resolution, that raise the mind to noble action.[26]

This image needs a little examination and analysis. First of all, it is a mythical image, because Antonio refers to the Trojan horse described by Homer in the "Iliad" and also by countless others. Then, what is more remarkable, the Trojan horse is usually taken to be a symbol that has negative associations,—a symbol of destruction but here Antonio gives an entirely positive interpretation and valuation of it. He himself is noble, so he thinks nobly of the entire affair. Ferdinand asks him his opinion of horseman-ship and he says he thinks it to be noble, then he uses the image from classical mythology. The wooden horse gave shelter to brave warriors who came out of it to win victory over their enemies. So, according to Antonio, good horsemanship gives birth to resolution, bravery and heroism. This is an entirely positive meaning given to an usually negative image. It is because Antonio himself is noble that he gives such a noble interpretation. He just cannot think of anything that is ignoble. No wonder that the Duchess chose him for her husband. He was the right, indeed, the only, possible choice.

His description of the Duchess is a succession of lovely images. Only two are being given here for convenience:

> She throws upon a man so sweet a look,
> That it were able to raise one to a galliard
> That lay in a dead palsy, and to dote
> On that sweet countenance.[27]

This is the first image he gives us and it calls for special attention because of the reference to "galliard". A galliard was a specially lively dance of the time. Antonio says of the Duchess that she looks so sweetly on a man that if he had been lying stricken by paralysis he would be inspired and enabled to dance a galliard by looking at her face only. The mention of the galliard makes this passage a specially effective one. It is a dynamic visual image. A few lines later, in the same passage, he says:

> ...her nights, nay, her very sleeps,
> Are more in heaven than other ladies' shrifts[28]

This highly praising, religious image is remarkable because it is inspired by a poem of Donne, "The Second Anniversarie". The specific lines referred to are:

> Whose twilights are more clear than our mid-day,
> Who dreams devoutlier than most use to pray.

So here we have a religious image, stressing the Duchess's purity. Indeed, he stresses her purity in more ways than one, for a little later he says again when he finally sums up her nature in a pithy line with another image:

> She stains the time past, light the time to come.[29]

This is an image that he used, in almost the same form in his "A Monumental Column". Here Prince Henry is said to "Stain the time past and light the time to come." This kind of repetition is a feature of his work as has been pointed out by F. Allen, the editor of the text that is being used. This is an abstract image, though it is actually a visual one, for two images are being used, the first that of a dark colour ("stains") and the second that of a light, that is, a candle or a lantern.

A few pages later in the same scene there is a very lovely image of a little child. In fact, there are two of them:

> the weak delight
> To see the little wanton ride a-cock-horse
> Upon a painted stick, or hear him chatter
> Like a taught starling.[30]

This is a delightful image, first of a child riding a-cock-horse on stick painted as a horse, with the face of a horse and then that of a child talking like a bird. Both are images having to do with a child. The first one is a visual image and the second is an auditory one as well as an animal image, that of a bird.

A few lines later there is a highly attractive image when Antonio says:

> There is a saucy and ambitious devil
> Is dancing in this circle[31]

He is, of course, speaking of Cupid, the god of love. This it is a classical mythological image, a visual, dynamic and very attractive one, as indeed it should be. It is a scene in which the Duchess is actually courting Antonio since she wants to marry him. She is going to marry him in the same scene a little later. But first she has to make him aware that she wants to marry him and this is part of that wooing-scene. It used to be, and it still is, the custom that no one can propose marriage to the sovereign ruler of a country as the Duchess is. She is the sovereign ruler of the state of Malfi. So no one can propose to her, she has to propose to whoever it is she wants to marry. In this case, this is specially difficult because though Antonio admires her very much, there is no thought of marriage in his head. He cannot imagine that she wants him. She has to prepare him for it. This is how she does it and he at last becomes aware of her intention and expresses it in this image. It is a specially appropriate one as Cupid is the classical god of love.

Another pleasant image in the same scene comes about a page later. The Duchess is contrasting herself with her marble statue at her dead first husband's tomb:

> This is flesh and blood sir,
> 'Tis not the figure cut in alabaster
> Kneels at my husband's tomb.[32]

In this scene, specially this last part of it, there are many fine and pleasant images in quick succession. After this, it is true, beautiful and pleasant images come farther apart and are fewer in number. Bosola the malcontent usually makes use of unpleasant images, but in next scene he gives us a very attractive one:

> I look no higher than I can reach: they are
> the gods that must ride on winged horses.[33]

By "winged horses" he is, of course, referring to Pegasus, the one and only winged horse in classical mythology, whose hooves brought the fountain of poetic inspiration, Hippocrene, into being. The image is thus a mythical one, an animal one (however imaginary it might be), and also, sensually, a visual one. It is rather unlike Bosola to give us such an attractive and entirely positive image at this stage, though later he gives us many, especially after associating with the Duchess has brought about a significant change in him. It is an instance of how Webster can create beauty in the most unlikely and, indeed, the most unexpected, places. He carries on this image of a horse, in a more ordinary way (that is to say, not mythical), in the next sentence:

> ...for mark me, when a man's mind rides faster than his horse can gallop, they quickly both tire.[34]

This is at bottom a pleasant animal image. It is a visual image and a dynamic one also, since it is about a galloping horse. Surprisingly enough, Bosola makes use of more of such pleasant images with positive associations, in the next scene. They come in a long passage, in which there are many such images, of many different kinds:

> The orange tree bears ripe and green fruit and blossom all together; ...The lusty spring smells well, but the drooping autumn tastes well. If we have the same golden shower that rained in same Danaës still, to hold up their laps to receive them.[35]

Here we have several beautiful images one after the other. The opening image is that of an orange tree that bears ripe fruit, green, unripe fruit as well as blossoms at the same time. That is to say, it is a nature image. To be more specific it is a composite image, of tree, fruit and flower all together, all visual images. Webster appears to have been quite fond of this image, as he uses it again in "A Monumental Column",

> But like the orange-tree his fruits he bore,—
> Some gather'd he had green, and blossoms store.

Next we have the image of spring-time, which is an image concerning a season and thus a nature image. In addition, it is an olfactory image as it mentions smells. Then comes the image about autumn, a nature image about a season and a gustatory one at that since it mentions taste. In the next sentence, we have an image from classical mythology-Danaë, beautiful princess, was shut up in a tower. Jupiter, the supreme god, the thunderer, saw her on the roof of the tower and came down to her, in the disguise of a shower of gold which she caught in her lap. So this is a mythological image, involving a well-known story and a shower of gold, that is, an image of metal. Therefore, it is a visual image and by implication, an auditory one also for a shower of gold makes a pleasant, tinkling, musical noise. This is a passage very rich in images of different kinds : nature and classical images, visual, olfactory, gustatory and auditory images. It is difficult to find a passage so-very rich in imagery elsewhere in Jacobean tragedy.

The next attractive image appears quite some time later, in the next Act. Ferdinand tells the Duchess that the Duchess has to marry a man with whom he has made the necessary arrangements. When the Duchess wants to know who this man is she is told it is Count Malatesti. She is derisive at this and says about the Count:

> Fie upon him!
> A Count! he's a mere stick of sugar-candy;
> You may look quite through him.[36]

This is an example of how our dramatist uses a pleasant image for purposes that are, at bottom, unpleasant. A sugar-candy doll is an attractive thing, specially for a child. It is something that not only a child but a teen-ager and on occasion even an adult might want, if not actually covet. Here, however, it is used for the purpose of ridicule, for a sugar-candy doll however highly attractive it may be for a child, is by no means a symbol of strength or of masculine charm. So the Duchess speaks of a man who is a thin one and can be snapped up, as it were, with two fingers—a derogatory figure altogether. All the same the basic image of a sugar-candy figure, by itself is an attractive one—a visual, tactile and gustatory image since such a doll is sweet to taste. This quality, indeed, is the very first thing one thinks of. He uses the same image in almost the same words, once again in "The Devil's Law-case."

There are several charming images in the next scene. Antonio disparages a single, unmarried life (whether it is a man or a woman), thus, giving instances from classical mythology:

> We see how Daphne, for her peevish flight,
> Became a fruitless bay-tree; Syrinx turn'd
> To the pale, empty reed; Anaxarete
> Was frozen into marble[37]

Here there are references to three classical stories. Daphne was an exceptional beauty. The god Apollo desired her so much that he pursued her though she did not want him and fled from him. She prayed to her father who was a river-god to rescue her from the Sun-god's lust, and at the last moment, just before her capture, was turned into a laurel, or bay, tree. This tree, thereafter, became sacred to Apollo. Syrinx too, was a nymph and inflamed Pan's desire and, on his pursuit of her, fled from him. She was turned into a clump of reeds. These reeds were later taken by the god and formed into a pipe from which he produced music. Anaxarete, by her refusal to yield to her lover, a mortal man, made him hang himself. This made Venus so very angry that she transformed this girl into marble. All such stories and many more of them are to be found in Ovid's "Metamorphoses" which was an easily available and popular book at that time. The images are mythological and visual, each involving a well-known story, and that makes all three of them highly evocative ones.

A few lines later he gives an account of the Judgement of Paris as it was, and is, still known:

> This was Paris's case,
> And he was blind in't, and there was great cause;
> For how was't possible he could judge right,
> Having three amorous goddesses in view,
> And they stark naked?[38]

The myth behind it, in short, was this: Paris who was only a shepherd at the time and not yet a Trojan prince, was known as a connoisseur of female beauty. So, three goddesses, Juno, Venus and Athene, came to him to make him a judge of their beauty and award the most beautiful the golden apple which was meant "for the fairest". That itself is another story and not quite relevant here. So Paris had to judge between them and did so. That is also another story and a long one because this is how the war over Helen started which is the story told by Homer. This story of the judgement of Paris is but the beginning of "Iliad" and in this place Antonio refers to it to illustrate the fallibility of men, specially when confronted by beauty as well as temptation, for all the three goddesses, not content with displaying their beauty, also tempted him, in three different ways, with might, fame and beauty.

The next attractive image is given by the Duchess, about three pages later, in the same scene. Ferdinand comes and rails at her and she says:

> Why should only I
> Be cas'd up, like a holy relic? I have youth
> And a little beauty.[39]

Why, indeed? But that is something which is not the concern of our study at present. This is a very attractive image—that of a holy relic. It is associated with religion and a holy relic symbolizes not just purity but inaccessibility as well. It is a visual image with holy, not to say divine, associations. It suits the Duchess admirably.

The next such image is an oft-quoted, a truly lovely one, and it is given by Bosola. He is speaking, indirectly of Antonio, praising him as an honest man:

> An honest statesman to a prince
> Is like a cedar planted by a spring;
> The spring bathes the tree's roots, the grateful tree
> Rewards it with his shadow.[40]

This is not only a fine, beautiful image, but it is also one of the best passages in the play. It is a very effective, poetic passage, known for its beauty. The image is from nature, one involving a tree and water, both symbolic of beauty and sacrifice, purity and harmony. It is full of implications of self-sacrifice, gratitude, and above all, of giving unstintedly of one's best. This is a visual and nature image of the best quality, expressed in a passage of exceptional poetic quality.

This is succeeded by another passage by Bosola in which pleasant images quickly succeed each other. A few of them are quoted below, the others will just be referred to. First he says:

> For you have made your private nuptial bed
> The humble and fair seminary of peace.[41]

This is a very fine image. A bed is equated with a seminary of peace. A seminary is a place for teaching. It is usually an enclosed, private place meant for educational and peaceful purposes. So this image is meant for education in sacred things ("seminary of peace") and an enclosed place, secluded from ordinary life. Again, this is an image eminently suited for the Duchess, associated as it is, with purity and also inaccessibility, for seminaries are not meant for common people. It is difficult to get inside them.

This is followed by one image after another, all extolling the virtues of the Duchess and of Antonio as well. (1) Scholars will pray for the Duchess, (2) the young girls who have no dowry will have some hope now of marriage, (3) soldiers will turn into Christians (that is, those who were not Christians already, like for example Turks) in order to serve her, (4) poets will thank her and sing her praises, (5) heralds will proclaim the praise of Antonio when they want to sell their coat-of-arms. All these different images are for enhancing the nobility of the Duchess as well as Antonio. They are, all of them, visual images and all concerned with the daily life of ordinary people, not belonging to the nobility, though taken from different walks of life.

After this there are but few beautiful images, for the torture and the death of the Duchess follows. One is given by the Duchess after they have been banished from Ancona. She says, referring to their miserable state:

> The birds that live i'the field
> On the wild benefit of nature, live
> Happier lives than we: for they may choose their mates,
> And carol their sweet pleasures to the spring.[42]

This is a very fine nature image, an image concerned with birds. It is both visual and auditory since their carolling is described. It has to do with mating also, so by implication love and domestic bliss is also involved.

As Bosola's character undergoes a change because of his associating with the Duchess, his images also change. The next pleasant image is given by him. He has grown to admire the Duchess for her endurance and fortitude and describes her thus:

> You may discern the shape of loveliness
> More perfect in her tears than her smiles[43]

This image of loveliness in tears and smiles serves to make the nobility of the Duchess clearer than a host of other images could have done. Bosola has given a perfect picture of her. The famous half-line image about the shining stars is also given by him:

> Look you, the stars shine still[44]

This image, as has been pointed out earlier, has been exhaustively discussed by the critics, and can be interpreted in two ways, both pessimistically, (signifying the indifference of the stars who go on shining whatever might happen to man) and optimistically. Since our present purpose is to point out the pleasant images in the play, this one can be taken in its positive meaning, that is, to imply that the stars (the gods) shine as a symbol of hope. As such it is a cosmic, a stellar image and a visual one.

The next beautiful image is also by Bosola. After the Duchess is dead he says:

> O sacred innocence that sweetly sleeps
> On turtles' feathers.[45]

The turtle-dove is traditionally an image of innocence and beauty, among other things and is therefore, eminently suitable for the Duchess, whom it refers to here. It is an image of purity and beauty as well as a tactile image since the softness of the turtle dove is also implied.

The last beautiful image in the play is given by Delio, an image of the sun:

> As soon as the sun shines it ever melts.[46]

This, sun image of one line, however, is not a very emphatic one and does not attract much attention.

Thus pleasant images are present there in the play, from the first scene to the last. As a matter of fact, they are almost as prevalent in the play as unpleasant ones. Yet paradoxically it is the ugly and the pessimistic images that have gained the attention of the critics. Perhaps they are the more emphatic ones, but it has been seen in the preceding pages that attractive and pleasant images are present throughout the play, though they are always neglected.

References

1. Fluchère, H., *op. cit.*, p. 167
2. *Ibid.*
3. I : i : 2-3.
4. I : i : 11-15, p. 35.
5. I : i : 51-53, p. 36.
6. I : i : 179-80, p. 40.
7. I : i : 55-56, p. 37.
8. I : I : 264-65, p. 43.
9. I : i : 311-12, p. 45.
10. I : i : 455-58, p. 50.
11. H.T. Price, *The Function of Images in Webster* in Kaufmann, *op. cit.*, pp. 225-26.
12. *Ibid.*, p. 227.
13. I : i : 106-07.
14. I : i : 498-500, p. 51.
15. Kaufmann, *op. cit.*, p. 248.
16. I : i : 13-15, p. 35.
17. I : i : 414-18, p. 49.
18. W. Clemen, *The Development of Shakespeare's Imagery*, London, Methuen '77, p. 78.
19. I : i : 435-41, p. 49.
20. Clemen, *op. cit.*, p. 94.
21. I : i : 50-54, p. 36.
22. *Ibid.*, p. 79.
23. I : i : 311-12, p. 45.
24. I : i : 11-13.
25. I : i : 122-24.
26. I : i : 149-52.

27. I : i : 201-04.
28. I : i : 208-09.
29. I : i : 215.
30. I : i : 394-97.
31. I : i : 405-06.
32. I : i : 447-48.
33. II : i : 95-96.
34. II : i : 98-99.
35. II : ii : 16-21.
36. III : i : 41-43.
37. III : ii : 14-17.
38. III : ii : 25-29.
39. III : ii : 127-30.
40. III : ii : 254-57.
41. III : ii : 274-75.
42. III : v : 17-20.
43. IV : i : 7-8.
44. IV : i : 98.
45. IV : ii : 350-51.
46. V : v : 124.

10
Poetic Style

Style is an extremely important aspect of our poet's drama and has been studied in detail. Not only does his style reflect his age (i.e. it is an Elizabethan-Jacobean style) it reflects his individual personality as well. In addition, the style has to suit the speaker. Not all dramatists can meet all of these demands.

These plays were written in a mixture of prose as well as verse and Webster's were no exceptions to this convention. The characters of the main plot who are usually noble by birth, speak in verse and the humble characters in prose. For example, the Duchess always speaks in verse though Ferdinand does speak in prose sometimes and Bosola often does so. The mad men speak in prose.

Poetic style, let it be remembered, has two clear-cut aspects: (a) diction and (b) versification. Both will be separately discussed here.

(a) Poetic Diction

There are many classical rules about poetic diction and the Elizabethans knew them all. In this connection, Horace's *Ars Poetica* is relevant as it gives explicit rules. He says that diction should vary according to the genre as well as the speaker. In drama the characters should speak according to their age, sex and station in life:

> It will make a great difference whether a god or a hero is speaking, a man of ripe years or a hot headed youngster in the pride of youth, a woman of standing or an officious nurse, a roving merchant or a prosperous farmer.[1]

This sentence is quite comprehensive as it takes in characters of all kinds. The divine and the human are distinguished. The diction must be adjusted to the many varieties of human beings, and their age, etc. can be taken into consideration. There are many layers of differences between the basic categories of men. Horace points out the difference between a lady and a nurse, and differences between a peddler and a farmer. These can be added to *ad infinitum*. Basically, he means that the diction must suit the speaker. In later Elizabethan and Jacobean drama the diction became highly specialized. As M.C. Bradbrook points out:

> The specific style for princes, for lovers, for clowns, was fixed.[2]

Again, there are some things the poet should always keep in mind. The diction must be realistic in accordance with the speaker and in addition it must be such as to be persuasive as well as moving:

> The Elizabethan dramatist's style is one of impassioned poetic rhetoric, the two commonest functions of which are to persuade and to touch the emotions.[3]

As Aristotle and later rhetoricians have pointed out, the use of rhetorical figures was a must. Aristotle thought it important enough to include it in his definition of tragedy, for he said that embellishments in the proper place is indispensable. The style might be grand, or middle or low, but figures of speech must be there. Ben Jonson, for example, uses characters from the lower orders as his main characters and uses the low style. In the same play, when Sir Epicure Mammon speaks, he uses the ornate style because Sir Epicure belongs to the aristocracy. But whoever might be speaking, Jonson uses plenty of figures of speech as is fitting.

English rhetoricians also followed the classical masters and recommended figures of speech. George Puttenham, the chief of rhetoricians has said in a sentence that has become famous:

> There is nothing so fitte for the poem as to be furnished with all the figures that be Rhetorical and such as do most beautifie language with eloquence.[4]

These are the basics but there were many other ideas about poetic diction that had been expounded by other theorists. Among them Horace's is the best-known. He even tells the aspiring poet to give new life to do old and out-of-fashion words, and also to use newly-coined words. Webster, as other dramatists, was familiar with these theories and had enriched his style accordingly.

Stylistic Devices

Stylistic devices can be of many kinds, as symbols, imagery and rhetoric. There are no important symbols in our play and images have been already studied. It is time for us to have a look at rhetoric or figures of speech in our play. For the sake of convenience examples will be taken from the first scene except in rare cases.

Simile is a very popular figure of speech and it is to be met with in the very first important speech. Antonio is talking of the French Court:

> A prince's court
> Is like a common fountain whence should flow
> Pure silver drops.[5]

Simile is a figure of speech that finds similarity in dissimilar things and here Antonio finds similarity between a court and a fountain. One of the most famous similes occurs in the scene in which the Duchess is facing torture:

> I am acquainted with sad misery
> As the tanned galley-slave is with his oar.[6]

Sometimes the comparison is a long one, taking several lines, and then it is known as a Harmonic Simile. The famous description of the two brothers by Bosola is one. It is in prose and not in poetry but all the same it is a harmonic simile:

> He and his brother are like plum-trees that grow crooked over standing pools; they are rich and o'verladen with fruit, but none but crows, pies and caterpillars feed on them.[7]

Next to simile is metaphor. They are very much like each other, except for the fact that in simile the likeness between dissimilar things is stated in words like "like", "as", etc. while in metaphor it is not stated at all. The reader has to understand it by himself. This is not only a favourite figure with poets and dramatists but rhetoric scholars also. They think very highly of it. One of the earliest instances of a metaphor in our play occurs when Ferdinand is taking to the lords:

> Methinks you that are courtiers should be my touch-wood,
> take fire when I give fire.[8]

What he actually means is that the courtiers should be like his touchwood, but "like" is omitted by him. He uses another a little later, saying to the Duchess:

> You live in a rank pasture, here in the court;
> There is a kind of honey-dew that's deadly;
> 'Twill poison your fame.[9]

He is here likening the court to a pasture-ground with honey-dew as flattering words. But the comparison is a direct one.

Rhetorical questions are very favourite figures of speech with dramatists as they add a dramatic quality to speeches. Bosola, after the comparison of the brothers with rotten palm-trees goes on thus:

> Who would rely upon these miserable dependencies, in expectation to be advanced tomorrow? What creature ever fed worse than hoping Tantalus?[10]

Rhetorical questions are questions that contain the answer within themselves. For example, the answer to both of these questions would be a strong "No one", but one does not have to answer them, the answer is contained within the question.

Exclamation is another figure of speech that adds to the dramatic quality in poetry and so is frequently used in oratory and drama. There are many examples of it in our play. In the very first scene Bosola uses it most effectively:

> O that to avoid ingratitude
> For the good deed you have done me, I must do
> All the ill man can invent![11]

Here it is used to express Bosola's mortification that he is forced to do something that is contemptible, but this figure of speech can be used to express a variety of emotions. Thus, Antonio uses it to express his humility:

> O my unworthiness![12]

A few lines later the Duchess uses it to express her own state of mind at having to propose marriage to Antonio instead of the other way round:

> The misery of us that are born great.[13]

Allusion is a figure of speech that is used to lend richness and complexity to speech. There are many kinds of allusions: mythical, classical, literary, etc. Sometimes the same allusion can have more than one aspect. This happens mostly in the case of classical allusion as the same one can be mythical as well as classical:

> What creature ever fed worse than
> hoping Tantalus?[14]

This allusion is mythical as well as classical, but one can have classical allusion that are not mythical like reference to classical authors. Thus, Ferdinand makes an allusion to a classical author:

> I am of Pliny's opinion. I think he is begotten by the wind.[15]

We find an extremely complex one when the Duchess proposes marriage to Antonio:

> here upon your lips
> I sign your *Quietus est.*[16]

If one analyses this reference he will find that it is a religious-cum-legal allusion as it is the usual phrase used to express that the accounts presented for examination are found to be correct. As has been pointed out earlier, it is also an image that foretells the future but that is a factor with which we are not concerned at present.

There might be an implied allusion also in which nothing is clearly stated but the allusion is so familiar to all as not needed to explain. Thus when the Duchess gives her ring to Antonio he says:

> There is a saucy and ambitious devil
> Is dancing in this circle.[17]

He is, of course, referring to the god of love, Cupid. The allusion is so well-known as it not need any explanation at all.

In this way various figures of speech, used to decorate the style, are strewn all over the play. Webster never uses them for decoration only or to heighten the quality of poetry. They are always strictly functional with him. They always serve a certain purpose—usually to lend vigour and a more pithiness to what the speaker is saying.

Versification

This is a very complex subject and cannot be explained properly here in detail. Only some very elementary features will be pointed out. First of all, as the student will be aware, Elizabethan plays were written in a mixture of verse and prose. The noble characters spoke in verse, except in unusual circumstances, and the humble characters in prose. It is only very rarely that this rule was broken.

The verse used in these plays is blank verse, i.e. unrhyming iambic pentametre. This is not to say that all the verse written was iambic pentametre. Innumerable variations were used. In fact, it is difficult to find a passage of any length that is regular blank verse. One such passage occurs right in the beginning:

> Is̆ like/ă coḿ/mŏn foún/taĭn whénce/shoŭld flów/
>
> Pur̆e síl/vĕr dróps/iñ gé/nĕrál/bŭt if/ 't chañce/
>
> Som̆e cuŕsd́ /ex̆aḿ/plĕ poi/oñ't néar/thĕ heád/
>
> Dĕath ańd/dĭseás/es̆ throúgh/thĕ whóle/lañd spŕead/[18]

but this is very rare. There can be many irregularities and variations.

For example, a line might have an extra weak syllable at the end. In that case, the line would be called hyper-metrical or hypercatalectic:

> Ă vé/rў fó r/m̆al Freńch/măn iń/youř háb/it̆
>
> ....
>
> Hĭs más/ter's m̆ás/tĕr piéce/thĕ woŕk/of̆ héav/eñ[19]

Again, a line might have one extra weak. Syllable in the beginning and then it will be called Acatalectic:

Y̆ou/ar̆e ẃel/c̆ome tó /y̆our cóun/tr̆y cleár/Ăntó/n̆ió[20]

In the same way a line may have one weak syllable less in the beginning or more and such lines also have their names. All these variations are introduced in blank verse in order to accommodate it to the rhythm, the rise and fall of the actor's voice in a natural manner.

Another way of introducing variety in blank verse is the use of stichomythia. This device means breaking up a line between two or more speakers. Thus, a line is broken up between two speakers:

Ant.: That I should write somewhat

Duchess: O, I remember[21]

A little later we see a line broken up twice, thus making three divisions:

Duch.: What's laid up yonder for me

Ant.: Where?

Duch.: In heaven.[22]

It can be broken up even more, but these are enough now.

A typical feature of Jacobean drama is the use of senecan couplets at the end of scenes. These are sometimes moral sentences and sometimes they sum up the message of the forgoing scene. Thus sc. iv. of Act II ends thus:

Though lust do mask in ne'ver so strange a guise
She is oft found witty, but is never wise.[23]

As critics have pointed out, Webster uses the "sententiae" to drive the common morality of the day. The famous last couplet of the play is a fine example:

Integrity of life is fame's best friend
Which nobly, beyond death, shall crown the end.[24]

Before ending the topic of versification, it has to be remarked that the most famous single line in Webster (and, indeed, in all Jacobean drama) has nothing to do with blank verse or iambic pentametre. It is the line Ferdinand speaks on seeking the face of the dead Duchess:

> Cover her face: mine eyes dazzle: she died young.[25]

It will be useless to scan this line. It does not conform to the rules of blank verse nor to any other rule. It transcends all rules and can adapt itself to the enunciation of any actor.

Now let us scan a passage to see how irregularity in the meter have been used to increase the dramatic effect:

> Ĭ am̆/nót mád/yĕt tó/m̆y cauśe/of̆ sórr/ow̆
>
> Th̆e heáv/en̆ o'ér/m̆y heád/seem̆s máde/of̆ ḿol/ten bráss
>
> Th̆e eaŕth ŏf flám/in̆g sul'ph/ŭr ýet/Ĭ am̆/ńot mád/
>
> Ĭ aḿ ăcquáint/ted ẃith/săd ḿi/sĕrý/
>
> Ăs th̆e/tánn'd gall/eў sláve/is̆ with/h̆is oár/
>
> N̆ecé/sŝitý/măkes m̆e/súffer̆/ con̆stant/lў
>
> An̆d cús/tom̆ mákes/it̆ eá/sў.[26]

This, metrically, is most irregular blank verse. It will be noticed that first line begins with a pyrrhic and is followed by a spondee. The two often go together. There are many trochees as trochees and iambs go together. Many hypermetrical lines are there. In spite of these irregularities, it is a tremendously powerful passage.

Now a certain characteristic of poetic style has to be observed. It has been remarked by A.C. Bradley in connection with versification in *Hamlet*. There, too, it is in connection with versification in *Antony and Cleopatra* that he makes this remark, therefore it is apparent that the remark is not directly connected with *The Duchess of Malfi*. Yet it is a very valid remark concerning Jacobean plays and can definitely be applied to the play under discussion. The relevant remark is this:

> The versification, by the time we reach *Antony and Cleopatra* has assumed a new type.... It is accompanied by a similar change in diction and construction.... It is also more concentrated, rapid, varied, and, in construction, less regular.... On the other hand, it is always full of life and

> movement, and in great passages produces sudden, strange, electrifying effects which are rarely found in earlier plays.[27]

He implies, after these few sentences that in *Antony and Cleopatra* we have the later poetic style of Shakespeare in its perfection: that it has gained in poetic depth as well as in being more amenable to the rhythm and diction of conversation. All this is perfectly applicable to our play and induces us to examine the poetic style of the play from this special point of view.

Right from the very beginning of the play to the very end, we see all the characteristics mentioned here by Bradley. The versification is rapid, varied, less regular, but it is full of life and movement, that is, conversational in rhythm and produces "sudden electrifying effects."

In the first scene, we come across many passages that are highly conversational in tone and construction:

> Ferdinand: There is gold
>
> Bosola: So:
>
> What follows? Never rained such showers as these
>
> Without thunderbolts i'the tails of them: whose throat must I cut?[28]

Here we can hear the rise and fall of the speaking voice, the rhythm of speech, of two persons, and yet it is blank verse, though rather irregular. There are, for example, no less than seven feet in the last line of the quotation, with another syllable added at the end, that is to say, two and half feet more than the standard five feet of blank verse. This is fully in accordance with what Bradley means when he talks about irregularity in construction. This is but an early example of how the verse adapts itself to the speaking voice. The part "Whose throat must I cut" is entirely extra.

The quotation has been chosen for another reason also, it will be noticed that as both Ferdinand and Bosola speak, there is stichomythia in it. This lends the verse flexibility, and this enhances its conversational tone.

A few lines later there comes a fine passage. It is one of those passages of fine poetry which is characteristic of later Jacobean plays and has got a little of that "sudden, strange electrifying effect" of which Bradley speaks:

> Take your devils,
> Which hell calls angels: these curs'd gifts would make
> You a corrupter, me an impudent traitor:
> And should I take these, they'd take me to hell.[29]

Here Bosola is refusing to take the gold coins which were called angels that Ferdinand is giving him to act as a spy. The lines are certainly "electrifying", because first of all we do not expect him to have such moral scruples and secondly because of the play on the word "angels."

We find another example of conversational rhythm in faultless blank verse, that is, iambic pentametre with the use of stichomythia as well:

> Duchess: I think this speech between you both was studied
> It came so roundly off.
>
> Ferdinand: You are my sister
> This was my father's poniard, do you see?[30]

If the lines are scanned, they will all turn out to be iambic pentametres. Yet the tone is entirely conversational. Ferdinand's question at the end serves to make it more so.

This first scene is full of instances of good conversational blank verse, specially when Antonio comes in. Here is a particularly good one, because it is conversational, has stichomythia and also classical allusion thrown in:

> Antonio: You have made me stark blind.
>
> Duchess: How?
>
> Antonio: There is a saucy and ambitious devil,
> Is dancing in this circle.
>
> D.: Remove him.
>
> A.: How?[31]

Here we see stichomythia, since a line is split up between two speakers. The lines are not perfect blank verse, which does but enhance their conversational quality, and then there is the charming image of Cupid which increases the poetic quality of the passage.

Then there comes one of those electrifying passages when the Duchess makes her intentions clear to Antonio:

> What is't distracts you? This is flesh and blood, sir;
> 'Tis not the figure cut in alabaster
> Kneels at my husband's tomb. Awake, awake, man
> I do here put off all vain ceremony,
> And only do appear to you a young widow
> That claims you for her husband, and like a widow
> I use but half a blush in't[32]

This is a wonderful example of mature conversational poetry. It is of high poetic grade and entirely conversational at the same time. The image of the alabaster statue enhances the warm liveliness of the Duchess as contrasted to it. Yet the passage is entirely conversational, not to say colloquial. The last few lines when the Duchess uses but half a blush in claiming Antonio for her husband are truly charming. In fact, these lines can hardly be paralleled for sheer charm.

We find another kind of flexible and conversational blank verse a few scenes later. This time also, when scanned, the verse will be found to be pentametres in each line, but it may not be regular iambic pentametre. It is remarkable because though it is fully conversational, the rhythm and cadence of ordinary conversation is not there. Instead Ferdinand is literally shaking with anger, however unreasonable this anger might be. He is mad with anger and can hardly speak. The dramatist gives this outburst in extremely flexible verse—not ordinary conversation, not charming lyrical conversation, but that of furious, demented anger:

> Ferdinand: I have this night digged up a mandrake.
> Cardinal: Say you?
> F.: And I am grown mad with't.
> C.: What is the prodigy?

F.: Read there,—a sister damn'd : She's loose
i' the hilts;
Grown a notorious strumpet.
C.: Speak lower.
F.: Lower![33]

This is a truly astonishing performance. Here the verse is almost regular, yet it can be made out that Ferdinand can hardly speak because of anger. He rarely even completes a line. Instead he breaks off and then the cardinal with two or three words completes it. Yet it is blank verse, and the tone is definitely that of a dialogue, breaking off, as indeed it should be, because of Ferdinand's anger. Writing such a passage proves an awesome mastery over the medium of blank verse, for its far more difficult to write than obviously lyrical or poetically beautiful passages.

We shall pass a few scenes, though they have got some good examples of conversational versification and come to the scene of the Duchess's torture. This is the scene in which the Duchess has seen the supposed dead bodies of her husband and children and is in deep despair. The dramatist conveys that despair in masterly blank verse:

Duchess: No, I will go curse.
Bosola: O fie!
D.: I could curse the stars.
B.: O fearful!
D.: And those three smiling seasons of the year
Into a Russian winter: nay, the world
To its first chaos.
B.: Look you, the stars shine still[34]

What a dramatic passage is this! The dramatist has to convey despair and anger, not resignation, in these lines; it is abundantly clear that he has done exactly this, and that most successfully. About the famous half-line spoken by Bosola enough has been said earlier in different contexts not need any more critical comments. For our present purposes, it can be taken to highlight the Duchess's despair for it can be interpreted negatively, to mean the indifference of the gods to human suffering. However much the Duchess might suffer, the indifferent or cruel stars will still go on shining.

The next example to be taken is one of the dramatist's best passages. It has been quoted and discussed at length by literary critics from all different points of view, specially from that of imagery. Words fail to convey its poignant quality, its wealth of associations and of sheer poetic power. M.C. Bradbrook calls these lines "the most Dantesque lines in Webster". The Duchess is talking to Cariola after hearing that madmen have been brought to her lodgings. They have not yet been brought to her presence, but she can hear the noise they are making. She is half-demented, herself, with suffering as it is, and she says:

> I'll tell thee a miracle;
> I am not mad yet, to my cause of sorrow:
> The heaven o'er my head seems made of molten brass,
> The earth of flaming sulphur, yet I am not mad.
> I am acquainted with sad misery
> As the tann'd galley-slave is with his oar;
> Necessity makes me suffer constantly,
> And custom makes it easy.[35]

In the preceding pages, this passage has been discussed many times. The effect of the image of the galley-slave, of heaven being made of molten brass and earth of burning sulphur—all these have already been pointed out. It is one of those passages of blank verse that are a little irregular to accommodate the rise and fall and tempo of the speaking voice and an electrifying passage to boot, in its poetic beauty and strength. Indeed, one cannot praise it too much. As a matter of fact, one is amazed and overwhelmed at the magnificent effect of its poetic beauty. The dramatist has reached here a height of poetic effectiveness which even he will not be able to equal elsewhere. It is a unique passage.

Bosola's passage in the guise of a bellman is again a unique one. Ferdinand has denied the Duchess the spiritual comfort given to every prisoner condemned to death by a priest who prepares such a prisoner for death, by hearing his confession and sprinkling him with holy water. In 1605, however, provision was made in Newgate prison to provide every prisoner condemned to death that the bellman of St. Sepulchre should deliver a solemn exhortation in lieu of a priest. Here, Bosola has taken on that function and delivers a speech in couplets. The last few lines of the exhortation are remarkable:

> Strew your hair with powders sweet,
> Don clean linen, bathe your feet,
> And (the foul fiend more to check)
> A crucifix let bless your neck:
> 'Tis now full tide 'tween night and day;
> End your groan and come away.[36]

This is only a travesty of the rituals really followed Actually she is being dressed here in sackcloth ("Don clean linen") and ashes ("strew your hair with powders sweet") like a penitent. But the crucifix is real. Bosola has done his poor best for her, tried to console her and prepare her for an ignoble, untimely and violent death.

It is an ignoble death from a worldly point of view, it is true, but her attitude ennobles it. Again, in entirely conversational poetry and diction, she meets her death:

> Pull and pull strongly, for your able strength
> Must pull down heaven upon me:—
> Yet stay; heaven-gates are not so widely arch'd
> As princes' palaces; they that enter there
> Must go upon their knees (kneels),—come, violent death
> Serve for mandragora to make me sleep!—[37]

This again is one of those passages it is not possible to parallel in beauty, nobility and poetic effect. It has been written in entirely conversational language, though the tone is a heightened one. The lines are broken and of irregular length to accommodate the voice of the speaker. Since it was the custom in those days to take young boys whose voice had not broken for female parts, one wonders about the child genius who had enacted the role of the Duchess.

Yet the passage is in blank were. This again is one of those passages that overwhelm the critic. This is conversational blank verse raised to such heights as it is difficult to equal.

After this comes that unique line by Ferdinand:

> Cover her face: mine eyes dazzle: she died young.[38]

Webster does surpass himself here. This unique line is a pentametre (though not iambic) that foreshadows the onset of madness in its broken rhythm. It is in completely ordinary language, yet for dramatic effect it cannot be paralleled. It surpasses many eloquent lines or passages in grandiose poetry.

We hardly reach such heights of glorious yet conversational poetry in the ensuing pages, though there are many passages of illustration of conversational verification in the later scenes, specially in dialogues between the Cardinal and Julia and between her and Delio. One or two remarkable instances can be given. Ferdinand, completely mad, whispers:

> Strangling is a very quiet death.[39]

About this line, (again a pentametre, though not entirely iambic), Rupert Broke remarks:

> The mad Ferdinand steals across the stage in the dark, whispering to himself, with the devastating impersonality of the madman, "strangling is a very quiet death" is a figure one may not forget.[40]

This line, it should be noted, is not a perfect pentametre, more or less iambic, and entirely conversational. In the same scene, a page later, we have the highly philosophical reflection of Bosola:

> We are merely the stars' tennis-balls, struck and banded
> Which way please them.[41]

The dramatist's development of blank verse in the direction of conversational language and rhythm has been studied, in the last few pages, from the very beginning to the end. We have found, in addition to blank verse adjusting itself to the rise and fall of the speaking voice, highly beautiful passages, philosophical ones, and unique lines depicting different kinds of emotions like despair, resignation, even madness. It is doubtful if there is another play that can yield such a rich harvest of different kinds of blank verse except one of Shakespeare's like *King Lear*.

USE OF PROSE IN THE PLAY

The use of prose is an important feature in Elizabethan and Jacobean plays. It is regularly used in them, but the use is restricted in many ways. Certain definite rules were there, and some are being enumerated below:

(1) Noble characters speak in poetry and inferior characters speak in prose.

(2) Noble characters speak in prose (a) when speaking to inferior characters, (b) in special circumstances as when they are mad or on the verge of madness.

Exceptions, of course, exist. Ben Jonson's plays are notable exceptions. The above rules, however, are easily applicable to Webster's plays. In the present play, the Duchess's nobility, that of birth as well as of character, is of so high quality that she never speaks prose, not even when she is half demented with sorrow. Indeed, it is then that she speaks the most sublime poetry. But in other cases, the above rules are applicable. The play is remarkably consistent in this. Prose passages occur throughout the play, from the beginning to the end, and it is a fact to be noted that all the characters, except the Duchess, speak in prose from time to time. For that matter, there are very few characters present in the play who are not noble. Cariola is one and Bosola another. Again here there is exception, for some of the most effective poetic passages are spoken by Bosola, as has been amply illustrated in the preceding pages.

The very first prose passage in the play involves a noble character. The Cardinal speaks to Bosola. But this is not surprising. It is, in fact, in accordance with the contemporary custom, because he is speaking to a man who is inferior to him socially. However, mean and ignoble a character the Cardinal himself might be, he is a Cardinal and Bosola is a released galley-slave, immeasurably inferior to him. In this passage, which is largely an informative one, the audience comes to know that Bosola had taken on the charge of murder on his own shoulders for the Cardinal and had served as a galley-slave for two years for his sake. Now that he has come back he expects to be rewarded for his service. The Cardinal, however, is not only a mean person, he is an ungrateful one too, and goes out, after speaking only three short sentences to Bosola. After that Bosola expatiates on the character of the two brothers in a famous passage:

> He and his brother are like plum-trees that
> grow crooked over standing-pools; they are rich and
> O'erladen with fruits but none but none crows, pies
> and caterpillars feed on them.[42]

The passage continues for some more lines, with Bosola continuing to rail over his own fate in having served the Cardinal. After this some of the Lords enter and speak in verse but as soon as Ferdinand enters with his attendants, prose is resumed. This is again according to custom because Ferdinand is talking to persons who are inferior to him. This is the passage that contains a fine description of a bird by Ferdinand which has been quoted earlier in connection with imaginary. Speaking of a bird of prey Ferdinand says:

> I am of Pliny's opinion, I think he was begotten by the wind; he runs as if he were ballasted with quicksilver.[43]

Pliny was a noted ancient naturalist and his book *Natural History* was available both in the original and in translation to Webster as well as his contemporaries. The image of the bird being supported by quick silver or mercury is a particularly felicitous one since it gives the impression of speed as well as of brightness.

This is the passage that contains Antonio's image of the Trojan horse. He gives a noble and positive interpretation of the ancient legend. Ferdinand asks him his opinion of horsemanship and this is what he says:

> Nobly, my lord: as out of the Grecian horse
> issued many famous princes, so out of brave
> horsemanship arise the first sparks of growing
> resolution, that raise the mind to noble action.[44]

This makes the reader think of Antonio's own nobility. The Trojan horse is usually a symbol of defeat and the utter destruction of Troy, but here Antonio has given an entirely positive interpretation of it. This is one of those rare occasions when he speaks in prose. Throughout the play, at all other times, except in a passage immediately following this one, he speaks in verse. His speaking here in prose is fitting, because Ferdinand has spoken in prose also, but it is a fact to be noted that it is the only time except for another passage right after this that he speaks in prose.

His second passage in prose follows a little after this, as he describes the character of the Cardinal. Perhaps Webster has given him prose in this passage because the Cardinal is a character who does not deserve poetry, specially as a person so noble as Antonio. Ignoble subject is being treated ignobly, though the character speaking it is an intrinsically noble character. It has to be noted, however, that whenever the two brothers are described, it is done in prose. Antonio's speech, in evident disgust is about a character who is totally disgusting, so he uses prose. The subject is not worthy of poetry. Except for these two passages, he always speaks in poetry.

Act II opens with prose which is continued for some time. Bosola is telling Castruccio how to behave like a courtier. But this is not so remarkable a passage as what he says to an Old Lady a little later. He speaks to her with quite unprovoked rudeness. It is perhaps because the dramatist wants to establish him as a malcontent that he makes Bosola speak to a lady with a rudeness which she does not deserve. As a matter of fact, Bosola speaks quite like a typical malcontent in this part of the scene. He speaks thus to her:

> To behold thee not painted inclines somewhat
> near a miracle.... There was a lady in
> France that, having had the small-pox, flayed
> the skin off her face to make it more level; and
> whereas before she looked like a nutmeg-grater,
> after she resembled an abortive hedge-hog.[45]

This story of the lady in France was based on a passage in Florio's Montaigne:

> Who hath not heard of her at Paris, which only
> to get a fresher hew of a new skin, endured to have
> her face flea'd all over?[46]

Whether the story was true or not (it could easily have been an entirely imaginary one), it was a well-known one at that time. This is followed by a passage which is largely a list of ugly, disgusting things which were used for their supposed cosmetic quality at that time.

After this Antonio enters with Delio and from their talk we come to know that he and the Duchess have been married for quite some time. Then he talks with Bosola. It is noticeable that in this dialogue Antonio speaks in poetry and Bosola in prose. This kind of mixture often occurs there in the plays of this time, with the noble characters speaking in poetry and the inferiors speaking in prose. But when the Duchess enters the dialogue is entirely in poetry with Bosola too speaking in verse though he speaks but little.

The next scene again opens with Bosola speaking in prose and continues to do so when an Old Lady who is in some haste (because she is attending on the Duchess who has started her labour pains), and has no time for him. It is here that we have the well-known passage about the orange-tree and the succeeding pleasant images. It is rare to find such a long passage of pleasant images by Bosola. As a matter of fact, this is the only time he speaks thus:

> The orange tree bears ripe and green
> fruit and blossoms all together.... The lusty
> spring smells well; but drooping autumn tastes
> well. If we have the same gold showers that
> rained in the time of Jupiter the thunderer,
> you have the same Danaès still, to hold up
> their laps to receive them.[47]

In this passage, fine images follow each other in quick succession. First we have the orange tree image which is a nature image. The idea seems to have been well-linked by the dramatist, since he uses it once again in *A Monumental Column*:

> But like the orange-tree his fruits he bore,–
> Some gather'd, he had green, and blossoms store.[48]

This is succeeded by the image of the spring with its olfactory image ("smells well") and then the gustatory image of autumn ("tastes well"). This is followed by the classical image of the golden shower. This is a well-known story of one of Jupiter's many love-affairs: Danaë, a beautiful princess, was shut up in a tower where Jupiter, seeing her on the roof, was smitten by her beauty and came down to her in the guise of a shower of gold, which she caught in her lap. It is the only time that there is a long passage by Bosola in which all the images are pleasant and evocative ones.

After this we have prose after a considerable time, in Act III, sc. iii. The passage is about Bosola. It is a short passage about him, by Delio. Again it has to be noted here, that even though Delio speaks in poetry elsewhere, here he speaks in prose, perhaps because he is speaking about a person who does not belong to the nobility. In this passage, we come to know about an aspect of Bosola that has not been revealed up till now. Delio speaks of him as a scholar who delights in studying obscure and curious things:

> —a fantastical scholar, like such who study
> to know how many knots was in Hercules' club,
> of what colour Achilles' beard was or whether
> Hector were not troubled with the tooth-ache.
> He hath studied himself half blear-eyed to
> know the true symmetry of Caesar's nose by a
> shoeing-horn; and this he did to gain the
> name of a speculative man.[49]

The passage, by itself, is eloquent of ridicule and derision, but all the same, all this "fantastical" study on Bosola's part has served its purpose, it has gained him the reputation of a scholar, which is exactly what he wanted, however "fantastic" it may have been.

We find prose passages next in the famous anti-masque of madmen, in Act IV, sc. iii, when the Duchess's torture has started. The Elizabethans and Jacobeans had superstitious as well as fascinated fear of madness which the dramatist has exploited to the full. This is a long scene, divisible into several parts and the prose continues even after the madmen have gone out. There are eight of them in all, though only four of them take part in a conversation. Their talk is inconsequential, though what each one says is comprehensible enough. But, by making the entire dialogue inconsequent, the dramatist has conveyed, quite successfully, the impression of madness:

> **First Madman:** Dooms-day not come yet! I will
> draw it nearer by a perspective, or make a
> glass that shall set all the world on fire upon
> an instant. I cannot sleep; my pillow is
> Stuffed with a litter of porcupines.
>
> **Second Madman:** Hell is a mere glass-house,
> Where the devils are continually blowing
> upon women's souls on hollow irons, and
> the fire never goes out.[50]

This sample is enough to show the inconsequential, illogical quality of their talk. The dramatist has, very skillfully, given the impression of madness through their dialogue, even if nothing else (i.e. their dress and acting) is taken into account. It is a very difficult feat, but the dramatist has done it by highlighting the inconsequent quality of their thought-processes. This becomes more pronounced when two speakers do not pay any attention to each other's sentences but talk completely independently of each other, as can be seen in the quoted sentences when the second madman does not pay any attention to what the first one had said.

After their dialogue, Bosola enters, disguised like an old man. This is the second part of the scene and Bosola's highly important speeches are in prose at first. There are two of them, both memorable. When the Duchess asks, "Who am I?", this is how he answers:

> Thou art a box of worm-seed, at best but a salvatory of green mummy. What's this flesh? A little crudded milk, fantastical puff-paste. Our bodies are weaker than those paper-prisons boys use to keep flies in; more contemptible, since ours is to preserve earth warms. Didst thou ever see a lark in a cage? Such is the soul in the body: this world is like her little turf of grass, and the heaven o'er our heads like her looking-glass; only gives us a miserable knowledge of the small compass of our prison.[51]

This is indeed a most remarkable passage. There is the image of boxes made by boys to keep flies in. Then that most remarkable image of a lark in a cage. It used to be the custom at that time when putting a lark in a cage to put, beside tufts of fresh green grass, a piece of mirror to reflect the sky so that the lark might think it was in the sky.

After this the Duchess asks : "Am not I thy Duchess?" and Bosola answers, again in a remarkable passage:

> Thou art some great woman, sure, for riot begins to sit in thy forehead (clad in gray hairs) twenty years sooner than on a merry milk-maid's. Thou sleepest worse than if a mouse should be forced to take up her lodging in a cat's ear: a little infant that breeds its teeth, should it lie with thee, would cry out, as if thou went the more unquiet bedfellow.[52]

Here again one image succeeds another. The first is that of the Duchess's forehead, then comes that of the milk-maid, then that of the mouse which is followed by that of the teething infant. Four images, all of them concrete visual images, and all are about ordinary domestic life—herein lies Webster's mastery. No Marlovian grand poetry but simple, ordinary domestic life, and that too in prose, yet the pathos is, if anything, greater.

With this scene Webster has nearly exhausted himself. What follows in Act V is nothing very significant. There is the scene that shows Ferdinand entering mad, falling upon the floor, trying to throttle his own shadow. There are many persons with him, the Cardinal, a Doctor and Bosola, among them. Nobody can understand the cause of his madness. He speaks in prose and the passages are not worth quoting; they are not significant in any way.

The next prose passage occurs when Ferdinand enters for a very short time, uttering that extremely significant line:

> Strangling is a very quiet death.

It can be looked upon as prose as well as a short line of blank verse. For our present purpose it may be treated as prose. Rupert Brooke's very sensitive comment upon it has already been quoted in the preceding pages in connection with conversational poetry, and there is no need to repeat it here.

The play is drawing to a close and there is only one more prose passage in it, spoken by Ferdinand. The stage, according to the orders of the cardinal, is dark and Ferdinand, the Cardinal and Bosola fight each other in the darkness, killing each other. Before dying, Ferdinand, still mad, utters one passage in prose about Pompey and Caesar, how they died, Caesar in prosperity and Pompey in disgrace. Then Bosola gives him his death-wound and he finally recovers his sanity and dies, uttering a senecan couplet which is not our concern here.

There are no more prose passages in the play, but we have come to the end of it. Of the protagonists, only Bosola is still living and he too is going to die quite soon.

It has been attempted here to present a study of the dramatic prose as written by Webster in this play, and it has been seen that prose occurs throughout the play. There is great-variety in this prose, for the dramatist tries to portray all kinds of emotions in it. There is nobility presented in the prose of Antonio when he talks about the Trojan horse and the other extreme, the absence of sanity in the prose of the madmen and in that of the Ferdinand. Indeed, Webster shows himself as mūch a master of prose as of poetry, and that too of all kinds.

References

1. T.S. Dorsch, *op. cit.*, p. 83.
2. Bradbrook, M.C., *op. cit.*, p. 45.
3. H. Fluchère, *op. cit.*, p. 152.
4. Quoted in *ibid.*, p. 159.
5. I : i : 11-13, p. 35.
6. IV : ii : 27-28, p. 100.
7. I : i : 50-53, p. 36.
8. I : i : 128-29, p. 39.
9. I : i : 304-06, p. 45.
10. I : i : 51-54, p. 37.
11. I : i : 274-76, p. 44.
12. I : i : 423, p. 49.

13. I : i : 435, p. 49.
14. I : i : 54, p. 37.
15. I : i : 122-23, p. 38.
16. I : i : 456-57, p. 50.
17. I : i : 406-07, p. 48.
18. I : i : 12-15, p. 35.
19. I : i : 3 and 10, p. 35.
20. I : i : 1, p. 35.
21. I : i : 358, p. 47.
22. I : i : 369, p. 47.
23. II : iv : 78-79, p. 63.
24. V : iv : 28-29, p. 137.
25. IV : iii : 258, p. 108.
26. IV : ii : 24-30, p. 100.
27. Bradley, A.C., Shakespearean Tragedy, London, Macmillan & Co., Ltd., 1960, pp. 68-69.
28. I : i : 246-58.
29. I : i : 264-70.
30. I : i : 325-28.
31. I : i : 404-08.
32. I : i : 446-52.
33. II : v : 1-4.
34. IV : i : 94-97.
35. IV : ii : 184-89.
36. *Ibid.*
37. IV : ii : 224-29.
38. IV : ii : 258.
39. V : iv : 35.
40. Allen, *op. cit.*, p. 154.
41. V : iv : 59-60.
42. I : i : 59-60.
43. I : i : 122-24.
44. I : i : 149-52.
45. I : i : 28-33.
46. Allen, p. 144.

47. II : ii : 14-21.
48. Allen, p. 145.
49. III : iii : 40-46.
50. IV : ii : 73-79.
51. IV : ii : 120-27.
52. IV : ii : 129-36.

11
Critical Reception

In his own time, Webster was accepted as one of the best dramatists of his day but the opinions are not available. It was printed first in 1623 and again in 1640 and again in 1678. This shows its popularity with the audience. But this is not serious criticism. Actually, he came into his own in the 19th century when Lamb's essay revived interest in Shakespeare and his contemporaries. It was not so much of detached critical interest as reverent admiration that animated the Romantics and the Victorians. Swinburne's poem is a fine example of their attitude. A few lines from his sonnet are given below:

> Thunder, the flesh quails and the soul bows down
> ....
> The very throne of night, her very crown
> A man lays hands on, and usurps her right,
> ....
> Rage, anguish, harrowing fear, heart-crazing crime
> Make monstrous all the murderous face of Time
> Shown in the spheral orbit of a glass
> Revolving Earth cries out from all her graves.[1]

This is a sonnet, not literary criticism. It is a poet's perception of a poet's vision. It was he, however, who pointed out that like Shakespeare in *King Lear,* Webster has drawn the picture of an entirely dark world as a contrast to the showing up of the flawless virtue of the central character. Swinburne describes characters such as Ophelia or Imogen as characters shining in darkness. The Duchess may be included within this category.

Serious criticism of Webster started in the last century. Again, it was a poet's perception that drew attention to Webster when Eliot said in his poem *Whispers of Immortality*:

> Webster was much possessed by death
> He saw the skull beneath the skin.[2]

By this time, with the horrifying experiences of the first World War behind them, literary critics as well as producers and theatre-goers discovered that Webster's desperate portrait of an evil world-order can be put upon the stage and understood. W.A. Edwards expressed the central mood of his plays:

> Events are not within our control nor are our human destiny, let us snatch what comes and clutch it, fight our way out of tight corners and meet the end without squealing.[3]

Different aspects of Webster's art began to come under critical scrutiny. One of the most perceptive studies is by Una Ellis-Fermor and another by H.T. Price. The former makes a comprehensive study of Webster from a highly philosophical point of view:

> His purpose seems to be to create, as rapidly as is consistent with fullness and depth, a picture of the world in which his characters move; a world created by their thoughts and of the deeds which are the outcome of their thoughts.[4]

Her studies of the plays of Webster are accordingly studies of the mood and atmosphere of the plays. What is more, she looks at the characters as a study of a single character, done in a series. For example, there is the character-study of what she calls the "politician":

> The group of "politicians", half stoic and half Machiavellians, begins with Flamineo in *The White Devil*... and goes on in *The Duchess of Malfi* to study separately the fitful, complex and inconsistent in Bosola and the pure intellectual politician, the incarnation of Machiavellian doctrine in the Cardinal.[5]

This philosophical attitude is visible in her treatment of the plot as well:

> The true plot of his play is not the event which proceeds upon the surface and are flung off, as it were, as a casual expression, but the progress of the minds of the central figure towards deeper and deeper self-knowledge.[6]

She analyses the play accordingly from the point of view of Bosola as a malcontent.

A very penetrating study of Webster's imagery has been made by H.T. Price who talks about his use of "figure in action" and "figure in words" and he studies the whole play of *The Duchess of Malfi* from this point of view. In his view these two kinds of figures reinforce and support each other and this is what makes his position unique:

> Webster's co-ordination of the figure in word with the figure in action makes his position unique in drama.... The only possible comparison is with Shakespeare.[7]

Another significant study of Webster is by Inga-Stina Ekeblad who takes one of the views of T.S. Eliot and builds her study around it. Eliot says that the art of the Elizabethans was an impure art as the Elizabethans aimed at attaining realism and at the same time kept within the highly unrealistic conventions of the day. She comments after giving the relevant quotation from Eliot:

> Obviously *The Duchess of Malfi* is an outstanding example of the "impure art" of the Elizabethans. Here, in one play Webster plays over the whole gamut between firm convention and complex realism.[8]

She then proceeds to analyse the play from this point of view.

These three essays are representative of three individual points of view of 20th century critical reception of Webster. All, in other words, accept his mastery in thought and character, language and plot and are of the opinion that the only one who comes near him in these matters is Shakespeare.

A product of inter-disciplinary work is given below. It is a study of the play in the light of the Sanskrit theory of *Rasavāda*. The work has been drastically abbreviated throughout, yet it is a study of this play from a completely different critical point of view—a work of inter-disciplinary criticism and as such is particularly valuable.

Some of Shakespeare's comedies have been studied in the light of *Rasavāda* but none of his tragedies, and certainly not one of Webster's. This is mainly because of the fact that *Rasavāda* does not approve of tragedies in general, as a matter of principle. That, however, is a different matter, one into which it is not necessary for us to go. What does matter, in the present instance, is whether tragedy can be truly appreciated under the principles of *Rasavāda* or not. One can certainly take up each scene and find different *rasas* in them as one goes along, but tragedy means that the end or *phalāgama*, will be dominated by *Karuṇa-rasa*. The enjoyment of *Karuṇa* is a much-debated subject and instead of going into the intricacies of those arguments, let us keep it for the last and try to proceed with the play itself. For the sake of brevity, the *rasas* are not being introduced now. Instead each will be tackled as it comes along. Not only the *rasas*, but each feature, like *rasa-virodha*, *rasa-vighna*, *rasābhāsa*, etc. will be dealt with as we come across it, though very briefly. The first few pages of the present work therefore will contain long explanations, but these will diminish as the work proceeds.

In the first scene of the first Act itself we experience rasa in Antonio's speech when he talks of a princc's court:

> Considering duly that a prince's court
> Is like a common-fountain, whence should flow
> Pure silver drops in general, but if it chance
> Some curs'd example poison't near the head,
> Death and disease through the whole land spread.[9]

This quotation is divisible into two parts, giving us the experience of two different *rasas*. The first part ends with the phrase "in general". Here, without doubt, we get the taste of *prakṛti-rasa*. This is a modern *rasa*, established by Acharya Ramchandra Shukla. According to him, its *Sthāyī* or permanent emotion is *rati* and the *ālambana* (fundamental determinant) is nature itself, it is not the *uddīpana* (excitant) as it might be taken to be. Here the *ālambana* is a fountain, though it might be an artificial one.[10] It pours silver drops, so it is definitely *prakṛti-rasa*.

As undoubtedly, the second part of the quotation generates *bībhatsa-rasa* (the Odious). According to Dhananjaya:

> ...the odious (*bībhatsa*) sentiment has disgust (*jugupsā*) as the sole basis.[11]

It has been divided into two categories, *śuddha* and *aśuddha*, and there are more sub-divisions. It is based mainly on physical reactions, but in *Nātya-Darpana* (Ramācandra-Guṇacandra, twelfth century) the authors have given a mental interpretation of this *rasa* and here definitely we have the generating of mental *bibhatsa* as we experience a mental disgust (*jugupsā*). In this instance, Antonio is the *āsraya* (recipient) of the *rasa*, Delio the *ālambana* (fundamental determinant) and the image itself is the *uddīpana* (excitant). After this, the Sanskrit terms will be used and not the translations, since they are brief.

The next few lines do not give us the experience of *rasa* though there are many *bhāvas* (sentiments). There are of many kinds. *Sthāyī bhāvas* correspond to the *rasas*, so we do not have to trouble about them. *Sañcārī* or *vyābhicārī* (transitory) emotions come and go. As there are no less than thirty-three of them, we shall not go into details. Emotions like weakness (*glāni*), fear (*śaṅkā*), envy (*asūyā*), intoxication (*mada*) are the first few of them. If, however, we trace their coming and going, the discussion will become too long. So, it is proposed here that only such instances will be taken up where there are *rasas* or something else remarkable, like *rasa-vighna,* etc.

Our next experience of *rasa* occurs in Bosola's description of the two brothers:

> He and his brother are like plum trees that
> grow crooked over standing-pools; they are rich
> and o'erladen with fruits, but none but crows,
> pies and caterpillars feed on them.[12]

This again is a case of *bībhatsa*. This too like the former example is an instance of mental *bībhatsa* where there is mental disgust that gives us the taste of this unpleasant *rasa*.

In Bosola's speech after this we see many *sañcārī bhavas*, the most prevalent among which are self-disparagement (*nirveda*), envy (*asūyā*) and weakness (*glāni*)

As for Antonio's description of the Trojan horse, here it seems that instead of the experience of *rasa* we have the opposite, that is, *rasa-vighna*:

> as out of the Grecian horse issued many famous princes, so out of brave horsemanship arise the first, sparks of growing resolution, that raise the mind to noble action.

These sentences occur in Act I, sc. i, just before the entrance of the Duchess. We do not experience *rasa* mainly because of two reasons, both have been given by Mammata in his *Kāvyaprakāśa*:[13]

> (i) *pratikūla-vibhāva-vigraha*, that is, the taking of opposing *vibhāva*. Here Antonio has done exactly that—he has taken the Trojan horse to symbolize nobility whereas it is the symbol of destruction, and (ii) is *prasiddhi-bhariga-doṣa* that is, going against tradition. Antonio has gone against tradition is ascribing noble associations with the horse. Instead of *rasa* we have *rasa-vighna*. It may seem to the reader that I'm being too particular in not finding *rasa* here. Let me assure the reader that *rasa* is not all that easy to find. Much labour is needed to create *rasa*. One will instead find other things that will be mistaken for *rasa* and it is the critic's duty to point them out, so that when genuine *rasa*-experience occurs there will not be any hesitation about it.

For many pages after this we do not have *rasa*-experience at all. Many *bhāvas* come and go. It will be wearisome to enumerate them. Let us take up the one where we have *rasa*-experience undoubtedly. It is the courting-scene in which the Duchess first courts Antonio and then marries him. Before this, in this same scene we have had opportunity for tasting *rasa* but every time it has not been achieved. Let me give only one example:

> Antonio: So please your beauteous excellence.
> Duchess: Beauteous!
> Indeed, I thank you: I look young for youre sake
> You have ta'en my cares upon you.[14]

Here, before *śṛṅgāra* can develop, it has been cut off. Again there is *rasa-vighna*. This time it is of the kind called *akāṇḍe prathanac chedau* by Ānandavardhana, Mammaṭa and others. It occurs when the *rasa* has not been allowed to develop but cut off (*prathana-cchedau*) untimely (*akāṇḍe*).

Now let us take up an instance where *rasa* does undoubtedly occur. The Duchess says to Antonio:

> Awake, awake, man!
> I do here put off all vain ceremony,
> And only do appear to you a young widow
> That claims you for her husband, and, like a widow
> I use but half a blush in't.[15]

Here, indeed, is undiluted experience of *śṛṅgāra*. How has it been described by the scholars? How has it been described by the scholars? I am quoting only one justly famous opinion, that of Viśvanātha Kavirāja:

> Vedyānatara-sparśaśūnyo brahmāsvāda-sahodara
> Lokottara-camatkāra-prāṇah keścit pramātṛbhih[16]

This *rasa* is untouched by any other knower, and equal to the experiencing of Brahman, the wonder surpassing all ordinary world is its essence; sometimes it is experienced by other sympathetic persons.

The quotation carries a sting in its tail: *keścit pramātṛbhih*, but of that more later.

Before we turn to an analysis of the *rasa* tasted here, *śṛṅgāra* itself should be properly introduced. It is the first *rasa* listed by Bharata. It is also known as *ādi*, *ujjvala* or *madhura*, its colour is light green and the presiding deity is Krishna or Vishnu. Here is a table giving its subdivisions:

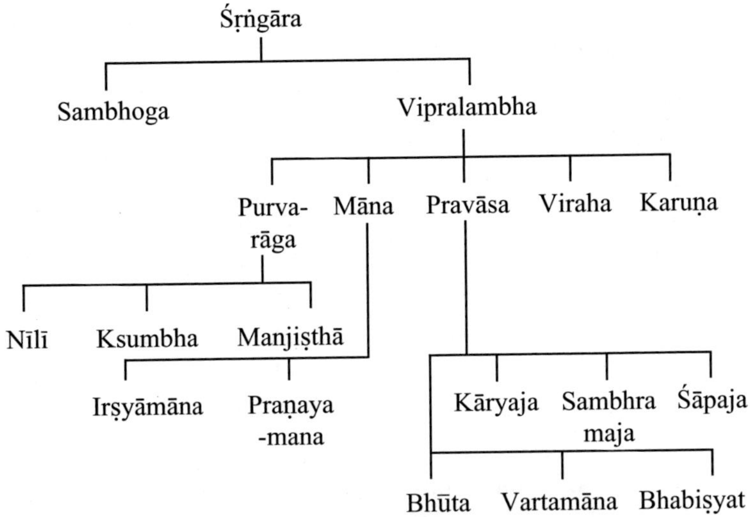

These are the basic divisions of *śṛṅgāra-rasa*. Again, different *ācāryas* have given more sub-divisions and have explained them. If and when we do come across them, they will be duly explained.

Looking at the passage under discussion, it is certainly not *vipralambha-śṛṅgāra*. Yet it cannot really be said to be *sambhoga* either, because though they are together, it can clearly be seen that the Duchess is not yet sure that she has got Antonio. She has to make him aware of the fact that she wants him and this is how she does it. So we can say that her love is still at the stage of *Pūrva-rāga*. As such it is of the *mañjiṣṭhā* variety. As can be seen from the table love at this stage can be of three kinds: *nīlī*, *kusumbha*, and *mañjiṣṭhā*. The description of these three different varieties will make it clear. We will take *Viśvanātha Kavirāja's* description of them:

> Na cāti śobhate yannāpaiti prema manogatam
> Tannītirāgam-ākhyātam yatha śrī Rāma-sītayo
> Kusumbhāragan tatprā huryadapaiti ca śobhate
> manjiṣṭhā-rāgamāhustada Yannāpaiti-śobhate.
>
> That fondness which makes no great show and which yet, when it has come into the mind, does not depart, they call it the Indigo Love—the Indigo being a colour that will well

> stand washing—such was the love of Rāma and Sitā. They call that the Safflower love which should but depart—Like the dye of Safflower, which fades in the washing. They call that the Madder love which does not depart and which does Shine.[17]

Here this is a love which is going to endure, and is very attractive in its expression. So it is *mañjiṣṭhā-rāga* all right. The Duchess is the *āśraya* of the *rasa* and Antonio is the *ālambana*. The occasion itself is the *uddīpana* of the *rasa*.

A few lines later we have the lines about the music of the spheres and the palms, spoken alternately by the two of them:

> Antonio: And may our sweet affections, like the spheres
> Be still in motion
>
> Duchess: Quickening, and make
> The like soft music.
>
> Ant.: That we may imitate the loving palms,
> Best emblem of a peaceful marriage,
> That never bore fruit, divided![18]

Now here again we have the taste of *rasa* and it is of the *sambhoga* variety. But there is not anything more to be said, because the *ācāryas* do not say anything about *sambhoga-śṛṅgāra*. But the lines are truly of high poetic excellence and successfully generate *rasa*. The characters are each the *āśraya* and the *ālambana* of the *rasa* and their being united in marriage is the *uddīpana*.

After this, again there is the generation of *bībhatsa* when Bosola talks to the Old Lady and it is *udvegī bibhatsa* as in two occasions before this. The Old Lady is the *ālambana* and Bosola the *āśraya*. The story of the lady in France is the *uddīpana*.

After this we do not have the experience of *rasa* for quite sometime, and when we do have it, it is an unpleasant *rasa*, namely, *bībhatsa*. Ferdinand is raving:

> Rhubarb, O for rhubarb
> To purge this choler! here's the cursed day
> To prompt my memory; and here't shall stick
> Till of her bloody heart I make a sponge
> To wipe it out.[19]

Here we have *bībhatsa* with Ferdinand as the *āśraya*, the absent Duchess as the *ālambana* and the news of her marriage the *uddīpana* of this most unpleasant *rasa*. After this is the bedroom scene, we have Antonio expatiating upon the unmarried state and giving many examples from mythology. This, indeed, is the last pleasant scene in the play. In this passage about the transformation of nymphs who fled from the embraces of pursuing gods, and the following,—that on the judgement of Paris, it can be said that we have the delightful experience of *adbhūta-rasa*. As we are meeting this *rasa* for the first time, and for the last time as well, an introduction to this highly pleasant *rasa* is needed.

The colour of this *rasa* is yellow, the *sthāyī* is *vismaya* and the presiding deity as Brahmā. It is of two kinds, *Divya* and *Ānandaja*. What is more important, it is the only *rasa* that can go with all of the other *rasas*, therefore there is no possibility of rasa-virodha in its presence. Nārāyana Pandita indeed, claims for it the status of *mūla* or the main *rasa*, encompassing all the other *rasas-sarvatryāpadbhūto rasah*. Viśwanātha Kavirāja, in his *Sāhitya-Darpaṇa* says that *camatkāra* (wonder) is the essence of all *rasas* and this *camatkāra* or *vismaya* (surprise) is the *sthāyī* of *adbhūta*. He quotes another ācārya who is referring to Nārāyāṇa Paṇḍita:

> Rase sāraścamatkārah sarvatrapyanubhūyate
> Tat-camatkāra-sāratve sarvātryapyad bhūto rasah.
> In flavour, even in every case, wonder is felt as
> its essence. Since wonder is its essence, it follows
> that flavour in every case is that sentiment or
> flavour called the marvellous.[20]

Now without going into any more of its intricacies let us look at the passage; only a few lines will be quoted:

> We read how Daphne, for her peevish flight
> Became a fruitless bay-tree; Syrinx turn'd
> To the pale empty reed......................
> ....this was Paris's case
> For how was't possible he could judge right
> Having three amorous goddesses in view.[21]

Here indeed do we experience *adbhūta*, and, though he gives us examples from mythology dealing with supernatural beings and from the story of Paris involving goddesses, yet it is not *divya adbhūta*, but *ānandaja* because we are delighted with what Antonio says. Here Antonio is the *āśraya* of the *rasa*, the Duchess and Cariola are the *ālambana* and the occasion itself is the *uddīpana* of the *rasa*. We experience wonder (*camatkara*) and surprise (*vismaya*). In a word we have the ineffable experience of *ānandaja adbhūta rasa*. This is the first and the only time that this is vouchsafed unto us—*Parasya na parasyeti,* etc.

After this, every time that Ferdinand comes we have the taste of that most unpleasant *rasa*, *bībhatsa* when he comes to see the Duchess in III: ii and gives her the poniard then *bībhatsa* is generated. As the Duchess is indignant and protests, we do not have *bhayānaka rasa*. She is not afraid of him. In this scene, we have an opportunity of seeing *rasābhāsa* for a short time. The Duchess says:

> Why should only I
> of all the other princess of the world,
> Be cas'd up, like a holy relic? I have youth
> And a little beauty.[22]

These are lovely lines, but I am afraid it is not *rasa* we experience here but merely its *ābhāsa*. This occurs when a *rasa* is applied in an indecorous, unjustifiable manner where it should not be applied. All the *ācāryas* agree about this:

> anaucitya-pravrtudtya ābhāso rasabhāvago.[23]
> –unjust application of *rasa* and *bhāva* cause
> *ābhāsa* of both, that is *rasa* and *bhāva*.

Panditrāja Jagannātha (seventeenth century) in his *Rasa Gangādhara* gives a meticulous analysis of this feature. He takes each *rasa* one by one. The only *rasa* he omits is the one with which we are concerned here, *Bhakti*. Now this was posited as not only a *rasa* by itself, but the main (*mūla*) *rasa* and all the others as secondary ones by Sri Rupa Gosvamin in his *Haribhakti-Rasāmṛta-Sindhu*.[24]

Here, I think, we have the *ābhāsa* of *bhaktirasa*, for we have the unjustified (*anaucita*) application of "holy relic" to a mortal, fallible human being. This is unmistakably a case of *bhakti-ābhāsa*. It is all the more emphasized by the indignant tone, unafraid, of the Duchess, as already quoted.

After this for a long time we have no *rasas* at all. Many *Saṅcārī bhāvas* come and go for scene after scene, but *rasa* is not generated. Then when in Act IV, sc. i Bosola describes the Duchess to Ferdinand we seem to have *rasa*:

> She is sad as one long us'd to't, and she seems
> Rather to welcome the end of misery.
> Than shun it; a behaviour so noble
> As gives a majesty to adversity:
> You may discern the shape of loveliness
> More perfect in her tears than in her smiles.[25]

These are very noble and poetically beautiful lines. But here also we have *rasābhāsa* instead of the real thing. It is definitely the *ābhāsa* of *karuṇa-rasa* because we have an unjustified appeal for pity for one who, theoretically, is not deserving of pity. She is a prisoner, and a prisoner is an ignoble person. Yet here nobility is being ascribed to her and we are being inundated with *karuṇa*. It is only the appearance of *karuṇa*, not the real thing. Since we do not have actual *karuṇa rasa*, it is not being introduced here in detail. Then for pages on end we have the coming and going of many unpleasant *saṅcarī bhāvas* like *nirveda*, *glane, śaṅkā, asūyā, dainya,* etc., each concerned with misery and despair.

But we do have undoubted *rasa*—experience in that famous passage when the Duchess says:

> I'll tell thee a miracle,
> I am not mad yet, to my cause of sorrow:
> The heaven o'er my head seems made of molten brass,
> The earth of flaming sulphur, yet I am not mad.
> I am acquainted with sad misery
> As the tann'd galley-slave is with his oar;
> Necessity makes me suffer constantly,
> And custom makes it easy.[26]

Now here there is undoubtedly the taste of *karuṇa-rasa* and the time has come to introduce it. Its *sthāyī* is *śoka*, the colour is grey and the presiding deity is Yama. It is of three kinds, *dharmopaghātaja*, *arthopacayodbhava* and *śokakṛta*. Here we have the last kind. Ācarya Dhananjaya has described it thus:

> Iṣṭanāśād – aniṣṭaptau śokātma karuno-anu tvam
> Nihśvāsocchavośrudita-stambha-pralāpitadah[27]
>
> –*Karuṇa rasa* is created from the *sthāyī-bhāva* of sorrow (śoka). Unfulfilled desire and misfortune are its *vibhāva* and sighs, stiffness, delirium are its *anubhāva*[28]

Sanskrit scholars do not approve of tragedies but in order to have the deep and undiluted pathos of *śokakṛta karuṇa rasa* we have to turn to tragedies. Not everyone, however, disapproved of tragedies. Bhavabhūti, the sixteenth-century scholar poet posited *karuṇa* as the main (mūla) *rasa–eko rasa karuna eva*, in his *uttar-Rāmacarita*. It is a very debatable point as to how can one enjoy the experience of *karuṇa*? It has been argued over by many scholars. We do not want to plunge into that particular quagmire. Let it be noted that the passage quoted above is one in which we have the undoubted experience of *karuṇa-rasa*.

After this comes the anti-masque of the madmen when we have *bhāvas*, and many of them, but it is doubtful if we experience any *rasa*. Then comes Bosola with his prose passage in which, again, we experience *rasābhāsa*:

> Didst thou ever see a lark in a cage? Such
> is the soul i'the body: this world is her little
> turf of grass and the heaven o'er our heads
> like her looking-glass, only gives us a miserable
> knowledge of the small compass of our prison.[29]

Here we have the *ābhāsa* of *adbhūta rasa* because we have the *anaucita* application of a delightful image for a miserable state.

Then, for a very short time, we have the experience of another *rasa* which we meet for the first time. The Duchess says to Cariola:

> I pray thee, look thou giv'st my little boy
> Some syrup for his cold, and let the girl
> Say her prayers ere she sleep.[30]

The pathos of these lines is unmistakeable but instead of *karuṇa* what we experience here more emphatically is *vatsala rasa* Viśvanātha Kavirāja has explained it thus:

Sphuṭaṅ camatkaritayā vatsalaṅ ca rasaṅ viduh[31]

As its expression is wonderful *vatsala* is also called a rasa.

This is not one of the nine rasas commonly accepted. It is a later addition as viśvanātha is a theorist of the fourteenth century. But *vatsala* has been accepted by all later scholars. Here the Duchess is the *āśraya* and Cariola the *ālambana*.

Then we have the famous beautiful passage by the Duchess—a justly famous passage:

What would it pleasure me to have my throat cut
With diamonds? Or to be smothered
With cassia? Or to be shot to death with pearls?[32]

I would be glad to say that we do experience some *rasa* or other in these lines but a purist will have to confess that, however poetically powerful and beautiful these lines may be, what we actually experience here is *rasa-vighna* for here the very opposite of the *vibhāvas* are applied. This is what Mammata has called *pratikūla-vibhāvadigraho*, the third cause of *rasa-vighna* according to him. One cannot be shot to death with pearls or smothered with cassia. Just the opposite effects are described here to what really happens.

Then the wonderful passage comes in which the Duchess kneels down to meet her death. It is difficult to say which rasa is tasted here. It might well be *śokakṛta karuṇa* but it is far more complicated for we are not just overwhelmed with pity but rather with admiration. Again, I think it to be a case of *divya adbhūta* here. We experience wonder (*camatkāra*) at her nobility. The Duchess is the *ālambana* and Bosola is the *āśraya* for he has genuine admiration for her.

Our experience of rasa almost ends here. Whatever comes after this does not have the strength or beauty to afford the taste of *rasa*. *Sañcārī bhāvas* come and go in all the scenes, these are strong also, but not so strong as to condense into *rasas*. At most the echo-scene might be said to generate *adbhūta* but since it is not either *divya* or *ānandaja* one feels at a loss as to how to classify it. It does give rise to wonder and might if one is not too particular be said to be a kind of *divya adbhūta* since it is generated by supernatural forces. Yet the echoes are not actually supernatural, they are fully natural so that particular theory does not really hold water. What we have in the echo-scene is popular superstition. So actually, it is a case of *rasa-vighna* of the second kind according to *Mammaṭa*, which is *kaṣṭakalpanā* or farfetched quality of *vibhāvas*. This fits the case exactly.

Ferdinand's madness which commences with Act V, sc. ii fills one with disgust (*jugupsā*) for more than with any other feeling. So it is a case of *bībhatsa*. Indeed, throughout the play Ferdinand's actions and speeches arouse disgust and therefore, *bībhatsa* again and again, till the very end. It is mental disgust or *udvegī* and has been mentioned enough times not to need any more repetition at this stage.

It can be said that Bosola's dying speech gives us the taste of a *rasa* we have not met with up till now—*bhayānaka*:

> O this gloomy world!
> In what a shadow or deep pit of darkness
> Doth womanish and fearful mankind live!
> Let worthy minds never stagger in distrust
> To suffer death or shame for what is just.[33]

There is definitely *bhayānaka* here, with Bosola as the *āśraya* and his approaching death the *uddīpana*. The rest of the characters are *ālambana*. But the *rasa* has to be introduced.

Briefly, then, the *sthāyī* of this *rasa* is *trāsa* (fear), the colour is black and the presiding deity is Yama. It has been classified into three kinds by Bharata-*Kṛtrima*, *aparādhajanya* and *vitrāsita* (due to fear). It is the last which is the case here. Bosola is afraid of his approaching death because of the many crimes he has committed.

It is only from the point of view of *rasavāda* that the play has been looked at and that too has not been done thoroughly at all. Only the instances of *rasa*-experience have been taken up and briefly at that. The plot, the character, etc. have not been talked about at all and the whole essay has been drastically cut short again and again. Yet, it is hoped, this inter-disciplinary analysis has added to our understanding of Webster.

References

1. Allen, frontispiece.
2. *Whispers of Immortality* in *Collected Poems*: 1909-35, London, Faber and Faber Ltd., p. 53.
3. Internet material on Webster, p. 2.
4. Ellis-Fermor, U., *The Jacobean Drama*, Methuen, 1960, p. 175.
5. *Ibid.*, p. 177.
6. *Ibid.*, p. 176.
7. *The Function of Imagery in Webster* in Kaufmann, *op. cit.*, p. 249.
8. *The "Impure Art" of John Webster* by I.S. Ekeblad in *Ibid.*, p. 250.
9. I: i: 11-15.
10. The translation is taken from Haas, co. transl., *The Dasarū pa: A Treatise on Hindu Dramaturgy*, MLBD, Delhi, 1962. The transliteration has been done according to the rules laid down by International Oriental Congress, 1894.
11. Haas, Co. *op.cit.*, p. 141.
12. I : i : 51-54.
13. Dwivedi, R.C. transl., *The Poetic Light: Kāvyaprakāśa of Mammata*, MLBD, Patna, 1966, pp. 357-58.
14. I : i : 362-64.
15. I : i : 448-52.
16. He is a scholar of the sixteenth century. The name of his work is *Sāhitya-Darpaṇa, Vimlā Tika*, pp. 48-49. Quoted in Dr. Nagendra, *Rasa-Siddhanta*, National Pub. House, 1964, p. 179. The translation is by the present author.
17. Mittra, Babu, P & Ballantyne, J.R., transl. *The Sahityā Darppaṇa or Mirror of Composition*, Bibliotheca Indica, Calcutta, 1861, p. 109.
18. I : i : 472-77.
19. II : v : 12-16.
20. *Op. cit.*, p. 41.
21. III : iii : 14-28.
22. III : ii : 127-30.
23. Kavirāja *op. cit.*, p. 44. Translation by the present writer.

24. Śrī Rūpa Gosvāmīn, *Hari-Bhakti-Rasāmṛta-Sindhu*, Pub., by Śrī Bhaktisundara Govinda, 847, Dum Dum Park, Calcutta 55, 1396.
25. IV : i : 3-8.
26. IV : ii : 23-30.
27. Dwivedi *op. cit.*, p. 240.
28. Translated by the present writer.
29. IV : ii : 124-27.
30. IV : ii : 197-99.
31. Kavirāja *op. cit.*, 3: 251. Translated by the present writer.
32. IV : ii : 210-12.
33. V : v : 97-112.

Some Important Passages to Explain with Reference to Context

Considering duly...whole land spread (I : i : 11-15)
Here comes Bosola...means to be so (I : i : 22-27)
He and his brother...feed on them (I : i : 50-54)
This foul...malcontent (I : i : 76-82)
Nobly my lord...noble action (I : i : 148-52)
He is a...heaven's knowledge (I : i : 163-73)
A most perverse...out of fashion (I : i : 174-77)
But for...rapture (I : i : 193-96)
All her...to come (I : i : 214-15)
Take your...take me to hell (I : i : 264-67)
Hypocrisy...will come to light (I : i : 311-14)
Ambition...all cure (I : i : 413-17)
The misery...woo us (I : i : 434-36)
Go go brag...love there (I : i : 441-43)
Awake awake man...blush in it (I : i : 448-52)
And 'cause...*Quietus est* (I : i : 455-57)
Whether...much of pity (I : i : 494-96)
Man stands...rich tissue (II : i : 56-65)
Rhubarb...wipe it out (II : v : 12-16)
Yes but I can...In tune (II : v : 53-59)

O fie...eminent stars (III : ii : 13-21)
Let not...own tongue (III : ii : 92-97)
For know...prince's favours (III : ii : 253-62)
He doth not...cunning (III : v : 29-32)
Nobly...she speaks (IV : i : 2-10)
In hell...loving wife (IV : i : 69-73)
I'll tell thee...it easy (IV : ii : 22-30)
Thou art...our prison (IV : ii : 120-27)
What would it...to you (IV : ii : 210-21)
Pull and pull...in quiet (IV : ii : 224-31)
Cover...young (IV : iii : 258)
Mine...die for it (IV : ii : 294-300)
O sacred...us hell (IV : ii : 350-54)
In those...bodies up (V : iii : 9-12)
It may...them up (V : ii : 343-50)
We are...please them (V : iv : 59-60)
I am...at me (V : v : 1-7)
O this...voyage (V : v : 108-13)
Integrity...the end (V : v : 128-29)

Some Important Questions

1. Attempt a character sketch of the Duchess in *The Duchess of Malfi*.
2. Explain Swinburne's remark that characters like the Duchess "Shine in the darkness".
3. Examine Bosola as a malcontent. Is it a true portrait?
4. "Even the inanimate world takes a part". Is this true of the images in the *Duchess of Malfi*?
5. Examine the poetic style of *The Duchess of Malfi*, giving examples where necessary.
6. "He and his brother are like standing pools". Is this a true description of the Cardinal and Ferdinand?
7. "He saw the skull beneath the skin". Is this a true picture of Webster's tragic vision?
8. Examine the plot of *The Duchess of Malfi*.
9. Write a note on the versification of *The Duchess of Malfi*, giving quotations from the text.
10. Write a note on the imagery of *The Duchess of Malfi*, illustrating your answer with quotations from the text.